Spiritism; the Origin of All Religions

SPIRITISM;

THE

ORIGIN OF ALL RELIGIONS.

BY

J. P. DAMERON,

Author of "The Dupuy Papers," "Devil and Hell," and "The Evil Forces in Nature."

SAN FRANCISCO, CAL.
PUBLISHED BY THE AUTHOR.
1885.

PREFACE

In presenting this little book to the public, I must ask the kind indulgence of the reader, for it has been the work of my leisure hours; a recreation of the mind from the dry details of law, which teaches us to deal with facts according to law, and to reason out its relations with the many conflicting, interests of mankind. In trying to trace out the origin of these laws customs and usages, it has led me far back into the night of time, when man emerged from the obscurity of barbarism. Like the explorer of some great river, as he ascends he beholds the stream branching off into many little rivers, and they grow less and less, until at last he finds its source in some far-off mountain, fed by the melting of the snows or springs that gush from out the granite rocks.

So it is with law and religion, they both come from the invisible source— the mind of man. One teaches him his relations to his fellow-man, and the other to his Creator; one relates to his social nature, the other to his moral and spiritual nature. They are closely allied and have much to do with each other, the religious status of a people having had much to do in shaping their government and civilization. Where a liberal religion has prevailed the laws have partaken of its nature and the people prospered and were happy; when illiberal it has tyrannized over man and made him a slave to caste and priesthood.

In all religions there are good moral precepts, and if man would live up to them he would be wiser and better, but his animal nature is so strong that it often tempts him to violate them; but they act upon and tend to restrain him. It is contended by some that man could not be governed without a religion. It makes but little difference what a man's religion is, if he be honest and will respect the rights of another. No one should say, "My religion is orthodox and yours is heterodox;" we should all be willing to let every one worship God in accordance with the dictates of his own conscience, for we are all in the fog and know but little of the life to come. We now and then catch a stray bit of evidence that goes to confirm us in the belief of the immortality of the soul. It comes like the whispering voice of spirits and angels, to tell us that we are immortal and will live beyond the grave. Is it our imagination?

Whence come these thoughts? Did we inherit them from the teaching of our ancestors? They had no better evidence of the facts than we see around us every day. They tell us these things happened thousands of years ago, in benighted Asia, among people just emerging from savagery, who had no knowledge of the arts and sciences, geography, astronomy, geology, chemistry, botany, biology, etc. They believed the world was flat; that the sun, moon and stars moved around the earth; that the earth was created in six days; that man was made of dust, and that God breathed the breath of life into him; that he caused a deep sleep to fall upon him, and took a rib out of his side and made it into a woman.

These infantile stories of the creation of man and the remarkable revelations made by God, are conflicting and bear upon their face the evidence of exaggeration and credulity. The evolution theory has swept from us the myth of Adam and Eve and the eating of the forbidden fruit in the Garden of Eden, which does away with the necessity of a redeemer and the vicarious atonement and original sin. It has opened our eyes to the knowledge that there is no one standing between us and our Creator; that every one must work out his own salvation and be his own savior, answering for his sins according to the law of compensation; that the laws of nature are unchangeable; that the same force that shapes a dewdrop will round a world; that suns and stars float in space, and are held in their place by the same law that guides the earth in its course around the sun; that spring comes to gladden the earth and make it green; that winter's frost robes it in a white winding sheet of snow; but the vegetable world is not dead, it is only asleep to blossom again.

Will man live after death? This is a question that has time and again been asked by the most learned sages and philosophers of all ages. Men have sacrificed their lives to prove it, they have been deified and churches and temples have been reared to honor their sainted names, and a vast multitude of humanity bowed down in their praise. Still it is an open question, and one that is hard to demonstrate. The only evidence we have is what Spiritism has been able to give us, but it is so conflicting that men of science differ as to the value of its evidence, and the only solution to the question is, each one must investigate for himself, in a spirit of fairness and candor, and he will find much that will convince him of the fact. I have examined the religions of all ages, and I find that it had its origin in the same intelligent force one hears in the mysterious rapping, the tipping of the table, the invisible pencil writing on a slate, the trance, the clairaudient and clairvoyant mediums, which is the only solution to all the stories we have read about gods, angels, ghosts and devils, that have ever manifested themselves to man; and the object of this book is to show that Spiritism is the origin of all religions; that all the knowledge of the life beyond has come to us through the same channel, whether it purported to be from gods, angels, saviors, prophets, seers, inspired men, or mediums; it is one and the same thing under different forms and different names, in different ages and different countries.

The object of the author is not to attack any religion, but to give a fair and impartial statement of FACTS, that will remove the veil that, for ages, has mystified man and shut him out from the knowledge that he is a part of the divine mind, and if he will but listen to his better nature he can hold converse with those who have preceded him, which will take away all fear of death and damnation and fill the heart with hope and joy.

J. P. DAMERON.

San Francisco, California, April, 1885.

CONTENTS.

The Rise and Progress of Modern Spiritualism.

CHAPTER I.

It is a New Edition to Old Religions; it is American and Democratic, and in Keeping with the Progress of the Age in which We Live.

"Rap, rap, rap, on the ceiling and floor,
On the pictures and door;
What is it that makes such a noise?"

All scientific investigations point to the fact that the earth was created by fixed laws, and that it was intended for the express purpose of developing man. For him heaven and earth have contributed all their best material, and worked it over well for millions upon millions of years, raising up mountains and eroding them down into the sea. Mineral, vegetable and animal life changed often before it was fit to be worked into man, the last crowning act of creation. In him enters everything, therefore he is a microcosm, his physical and intellectual powers are the perfection of nature and the pride of the all wise master.

Is it reasonable, yea, is it possible that all this should be done to make a superior animal who should eat, drink and use all the bountiful stores that nature had provided in building up the globe as a fit habitation for him that he should die and his body return to dust from whence it sprang; if so creation is a grand failure, and should there be no soul survive death, or was it intended that out of him should spring another form that would retain the knowledge and the individual identity in a more sublimated condition, capable of further progress. I see nothing indicating that mind—intelligence —can be destroyed or annihilated any more than that of force and matter, which has produced him. Then this intelligence must exist in an individual form, and that form must begin in another. On the investigation of the phenomena of modern Spiritualism I am forced to ad-

mit that there it nothing in it that is contrary to the fixed laws of evolution—but it throws new light on the *life-forces* of *the universe* called life, soul and spirit.

There should be no conflict between science and religion. While science deals in facts that are demonstrable to the five senses, and is aided by observation, comparison and deduction from which a knowledge of phenomena and of the order of succession is derived. Spiritism offers to lend its aid and assist science to explore those hidden realms of metaphysics and with the higher developed senses of clairaudience and clairvoyance which the academy of science at Paris has called the sixth sense, so with this higher development they will be able to go farther into the workings of the human mind and bring to light that hidden force called spirit, the life force of the universe that has caused matter to evolve and work out so many changes and forms in the physical world. As each atom of matter is accompanied by certain force or intelligence that cause that particle of matter to attract or repel other particles of matter, so that it knows its affinities and repels its dislikes; it forms the minerals in crystals, cubes, cones and prisms, for all matter is moved and governed by certain laws that are acting and reacting throughout the visible and invisible world and the invisible forms of matter are the most active and numerous; yet because we can not reach or comprehend these operations of matter with the five senses we cannot say it does not exist or move, but reason aided by observation and comparison is forced to admit the fact. We cannot see, feel or hear the iron crystalize but we are satisfied that it does under certain conditions, so there is a silent work ever going on in the secret laboratory of nature that is beyond the keen perception or understanding of the man of science, but which is revealed to the higher developed senses of the disembodied spirits and to those mediums that occupy a border land

So science should cease its hostility and cultivate that intuitional sense of the inner man (the spirit) which, if properly understood and trained, would aid it in the great work of arriving at the *truth*, which would lead to a higher civilization and amelioration of the human race by expanding the intellect in the direction of the spiritual, for the heart must be cultivated as well as the head, for the inner man has much to do with the outer man And until science and Spiritualism, physics and metaphysics go hand in hand the highest attainments will not be reached As Joliet says, "while the Western Nations have been following the physical laws, the Hindoo fakirs have been following the metaphysical laws of the spirit, by which they can control and perform wonderful things that startle the European with wonder and amazement, while we can by our knowledge perform wonders that are as startling to them "

That mind and matter, physics and metaphysics are all united in man and that he should investigate one as well as the other, that there is no dividing line, that it is the ignorance of science of these metaphysical laws that shut the door in the face of the pursuer of knowledge, and all that is required is to knock and it shall be opened; that man is the beginning of our individualized intelligence that never dies but follows the laws of progress through endless realms; that there is no end or limit to knowledge in this life or the higher life to come in the spirit land; that there is no secret in nature's laws beyond the reach of individualized intelligence of the aspiring mind.

Science, proud of her attainments and justly so, strong in her foundations of laws and unassailable in her primal principles, has nevertheless arrogated to herself more rights than she actually possesses, and claims not only to dictate to man the essential properties and elements that constitute the physical body, but here it shuts the door against any investigation of that which belongs to his spiritual nature

The result is that materialism is closely encroaching upon the church and is fast undermining and destroying the spiritual faith of the inner man and reducing him down to a piece of clay, destitute of any spirituality, while the churches are divided and making war on Modern Spiritualism, and invoke the aid of science to demonstrate the fact that it is all a delusion, at the same time proving to the world that all religion is nothing but a deception; for if there are no spirits for the Spiritualists there can be none for the churches

The greatest difficulty in describing that which relates to man's spiritual nature is the absolute ignorance of humanity concerning its nature. The spiritual laws have heretofore been ignored; the power of one mind upon another, the influence of spirit upon spirit, have scarcely been considered, while that spiritual power by which Jesus wrought miracles and spells (and also his disciples), which he promised should be given to all who believed and followed in him, has been wholly blotted out and tabooed by the church, and any attempt to revive it is denounced as the work of the devil, so that religion has come to mean a simple statement, a form, a ceremony, a theory, without any intermediate links connecting it with the world of causes and human existence, whereas in the time of Jesus it was a matter of daily life and experience and was so understood and practiced by him and his disciples The spirit was the great motor power by which these miracles were performed.

The working of spiritual gifts has ceased because they have been ignored by the church, and the temporal power and material influence of civilization, which has encouraged a growth of materialism. Prosperity, the building up of states, endowing institutions, the rearing of splendid structures and churches, goes far to build up the material welfare of nations and society, but they take away from the mind those absolute conditions that are essential to the existence of spiritual gifts—simplicity, naturalness, dependence upon the unseen and the recognition of the higher nature of the spirits in all that belongs to daily life. In following the material, man has lost much of the spiritual power that the ancients had. Though he has made great progress in the physical laws of nature in the discovery of steam and electricity, he has lost sight of the more subtle psychical force of mind over matter, which enabled the ancients to divine the future and tell the past It has well nigh cut humanity off from all religions and made him a materialist.

The Leading Scientists are Divided—Some are Materialists, others are Avowed Spiritualists.

Darwin could not see anything behind blind matter, forcing up the vegetable and animal life, but the "survival of the fittest." Herbert Spencer thinks that matter is impelled by the active forces in nature to evolve all forms of life according to its environments; Huxley admits that there is an "unknowable" force back of or in the atom that impells it to assume certain forms Agassiz thought all matter was impelled by an invisible intelligence, but would not admit that it was done by the spirit forces, still he believed in a GOD—a Supreme First Cause—that caused all matter to evolve under certain laws While, on the other hand, we have the illustrious names of Alexander Aksakoff, Robert Chambers Hiram Corson, Augustus de Morgan, J. W. Edmonds, Dr. Elliotson, I. H Fichte, Zollner, Prof Ulrici of Halle, Camille Flammaron, Herman Goldschmidt, Dr. Hoffle, Robert Hare, Lord Lyndhurst, Robert Dale Owen, Victor Hugo, W. M Thackeray, T. A. Trollope, Alfred Russel Wallace (a naturalist and scientist, a cotemporary with Darwin), Nicholas Wagner, Archbishop Whately, Pasteur, the author of the germ theory, and Professor Crookes, who stand high in science and learning, all are firm believers in Spiritism, and that the departed from this life live, can and do return and hold communication with mortals. These men have placed the mediums under the strictest test. Profs Wallace, Crookes and Zollner took the mediums to their own homes and placed them under the strictest test conditions On one occasion Mr Varley, the electrician, by means of a galvanic battery and cable-testing apparatus, showed to the satisfaction of all present, that the medium was inside of the cabinet, while the supposed spirit form was visible and moving outside. Prof. Crookes says· "It was a common thing for the seven or eight of us in the laboratory to see Miss Cook (the medium) and "Kate" (the spirit) at the same time under the full blaze of the electric light." William Crookes, after making many tests with such mediums as D. D. Home, Kate Fox, and others, says that "the spirits can move heavy bodies That they can make sounds and raps; that they can alter the weight of bodies, and move bodies when at a distance from the medium; raise tables and chairs off the ground; the levitation of human beings; luminous appearances, the appearance of hands writing; phantom forms and faces."

SPIRITISM IS AS OLD AS THE HISTORY OF MAN.

It appeared to Adam in the Garden of Eden; it directed Noah how to build the ark; Moses saw it in the burning bush, the spirits (angels) often appeared to Abraham, and at one time ate veal cutlets with him in his tent, Saul saw the spirit (or ghost) of Samuel at the Witch of Endor, the spirit closed the mouth of the lion when Daniel was thrown into the lion's den; Jesus saw Moses and Elias on the mount of transfiguration, and they talked with him; St. Paul heard voices and was liberated from prison by them, St. John had trances and saw the New Jerusalem Take the Spiritualism out of the Bible and it would be a tame, dull history of the Jews; but read through the light of Spiritualism it is full of interest and grandeur.

Spiritism is the basis of all religions and the only way man has got any knowledge of a future existence. It manifested itself in the Delphic oracles as well as to the Hebrew prophets, if we are to believe the Greek authors Socrates says he received all his knowledge from his little demon (spirit) that whispered it into his ears. The Platonic philosophy was but little different from that of Modern Spiritualism Homer is one grand poem of the gods (spirits) taking a deep interest in the affairs of nations and individuals The Greeks lived close to nature and held communion through the oracles with departed heroes and sages The Romans had their sybaline books and vestal virgins, who held communion with the dead. Cicero was a firm believer in the spirits, and was a medium; his orations burn with the fire of inspiration.

Every age has had its spiritual manifestations, every period has witnessed something of the kind, every fireside has its ghost story, and every family has something of its wonders to relate It is nothing new. In the year 364, in the reign of the Roman emperor Valens, mediums conversed by the means of rappings and employed the alphabet, as also the spirit pendulum It finally passed into disrepute as a black art and was denounced by the priests as the doings of the devil Independent slate writing was known to the Chinese over a thousand years ago. Trance mediums were known to the ancient Hindoos, Persians and Greeks, so was that of healing, clairaudience and clairvoyance; they saw and heard spirits

Christ was a medium of the highest order, he made his appearance to battle against the materialism of his day; he was invested with wonderful power to convince the wicked world that he was sent from God to teach reformation, but they would not believe him but crucified him. Luther had wonderful mediumistic power. He saw spirits and threw an inkstand at the head of an evil one The Rosicrucians were invested with wonderful power and were scoffed at by the materialists as fanatics They led a most singularly isolated, pure life The Huguenots were persecuted on account of their spiritual dissensions from the Catholic church. The Quakers, whose leaders were George Fox and others, claimed a revelation from the divine mind William Penn, the founder of Pennsylvania, was one of its followers The Shakers, an advanced class of Quakers, so called from their shaking and nervous twitching They were led to follow their peculiar life of celibacy from the teachings of Ann Lee.

In the more modern times it manifested itself in Caines and Marvels in France in 1686. Swedenborg alleges that he was in full and open communication with the spirit world, and daily conversed with spirits and angels.

In 1829, the Seeress of Prevost startled the world with what she saw, and mysterious raps were often heard around her

In 1830 the French mesmerists Billot and Deleuze say they saw and felt spirits, and there was a possibility of communicating with them.

Modern Spiritualism had its origin in the rappings of the Fox sisters and in the writings of A J Davis, who published "Nature's Divine Revelations; a Voice to Mankind," in July, 1847, in which he enunciated the doctrine of evolution ten years prior to that of Darwin

About the same time in the little village of Hydesville, N. Y., in a small, unpretending dwelling lived Mr Fox, his wife and two daughters Kate, the youngest, about 9 years old, was the first medium to detect and recognize the raps, which for some time amazed the family With the assistance of her mother she was she first to establish a system of signals by raps, though they had been heard often by different persons

Rev John Wesley's daughters were similarly annoyed by a spirit who answered to the name of "Old Jeff," but Wesley requested it to leave and let his children alone, at last it disappeared, and he lost the golden opportunity to make the discovery But the manifestation of the spirit attended his religious revivals in another form—that of shouting

It is not a religion covered with moss and rust of past ages, but one that is fresh and new in keeping with the progress of the age

IT IS STRICTLY AMERICAN AND DEMOCRATIC,

It has no synods, conferences or ecumenical councils, to fix up creeds and dogmas to declare what is the word of God It has no priests, bishops or popes, to grant absolutions and forgive sins It has no head or leader. The medium may be a child uneducated, if the communications don't bear the strictest scrutiny and test they are rejected. Every one is the judge, none being required to believe unless they wish, all are at liberty to criticize and comment whether it is truthful or false. The spirit is cross-questioned and examined, and if it don't stand the test it is discarded It denounces all leadership, all individual *man worshipping*, making every believer rely solely on himself and seek his own salvation through his own exertions. It teaches individuality—*"I am a man and you are another."* Every individual is his own priest; if he has sins he must confess them to himself, and he must work out his own salvation. It believes in good works; short prayers, for God is not captured by eloquent words and long prayers, but is pleased with a pure heart and a forgiving disposition. Good deeds and kind words are worth a thousand prayers.

It is little over a quarter of a century old, but now numbers over 25,000,000 of believers, making way amongst the most intelligent and wealthy classes—emperors, kings and queens. Though not demonstrative it is undermining all the older forms of religion that had their origin in the night of the past. It is a religion that is making rapid progress with the intelligent and thinking masses, for it is in accord with science and the laws of evolution. It carries conviction to all who will investigate it with candor and honesty of purpose. To the fair-minded man who is not steeped in prejudices of the old theology, there is evidence given, if he will examine, to convince him that there is an invisible individual intelligence that sees and understands him and lets him know that his departed friends are not dead but present and holding converse with him. The severest tests are given, that no one can explain save that it is the spirit of a departed acquaintance, friend, mother, father, brother, wife or child.

Man needs not external revelations but an internal illumination whereby he can understand the relations he sustains to himself, his brother man and the physical world. Such an illumination is bestowed on, though not perceived by all; that myriad hosts of the angel world are around us; they mingle in the affairs of men; their atmosphere is an exhaustless fountain from which we draw our thoughts and aspirations.

CHAPTER II.

OCCULTISM.

A Hidden Force in Nature called the Astral Light, The Soul of the World, The Primum Mobile, the Grand Arcanum of Transcendental Magic, The Tetragrammaton of the Hebrews, The Thot of the Egyptians, The Azoth of the Alchemist, The Akasa of the Hindoos, The Secret lost to the Masonic Fraternity in the Murder of Grand Master Hiram Abiff, Theopæ, Destiny, Occult Fraternity

" The power of thought, the magic of the mind "—BYRON

Cicero was of the opinion that the Chaldeans were among the oldest magicus, who placed the basis of all magic in the inner powers of man's soul, and by the discernment of magic properties in plants, minerals and animals   By their aid they performed the most wonderful " miracles "   Magic was their religion, and synonymous with science.

The influence of magic may be traced in the legends of Prometheus, Sisyphus, Circle and Medea   The Greek and Roman mythologies are full of it, and they had implicit faith in their oracles, auguries and divinations   The mythologies of the ancient Germans, Slavs and Celts were similar   The Druids also possessed the secret art   The crusaders looked upon magic as the peculiar ally of the infidels

In the fourteenth century magic arose into repute as a lawful art, and sovereigns maintained magicians at their courts.   The most prominent of these European magicians, adepts and writers was Albertus Magnus, Roger Bacon, Arnoldus de Villanova, Daniel Defoe and Eliphas Levi, of the present century

The arts of magic are founded upon the theory that there is an occult force in nature called the astral light, the soul of the world, and the *primum mobile*, which is the grand arcanum of *transcendental magic*, the Tetagrammaton of the Hebrews, the Azoth of the Alchemist, the Thot of the Egyptians, and the Akasa of the Hindoos   By this element, which abounds in the celestial bodies and descends in the rays of the stars, every occult property is conveyed into herbs, stones, metals and minerals, making them solary, lunary, jovial, ethereal, mercurial, etc , according to the planetary influences   *   *
In it thoughts are realized, and images of past persons and things are preserved, so that specters may be evoked from it, and shown to the world as real objects and things—as sounds and words are preserved in the audiphone

The adepts in magic claim that the sorcerer, or practicer of the black art, differs from the true magician as the charlatan from the master of the art, that the former invokes and uses the evil force or bad spirits, while the true magician uses the good force or good spirits   According to the teachings of Cornelius Agrippa, there are several kinds of magic, but they are generally reduced to two white or divine magic, or magic within its proper province, and black or infernal magic, to which belong chiromancy, the evil eye, the command of the elements (of evil), the power of transforming human beings into animals, etc   In the black, the magician sells himself to the devil; in the white, the devil is controlled and obsessed by the magician

To have command of this element, to direct its currents and to discern its moving panorama, is the highest attainment, and the incomprehensible secret of the magician. To reveal it is to lose it; to impart it even to a disciple is to abdicate in his favor. To command this force and its secrets requires the highest and best as well as the purest intellect, dauntless courage and unbending will, discretion, devotion, and habitual silence, and to be free from temptations. He must be chaste, sober, disinterested, inaccessible, free from prejudice and passions, and without physical defect. He must live a life of abstinence, having certain hours for meditation. He must make physical wants yield to those of the mind; he must be able to live on the scantiest diet, barely enough to keep soul and body together, like the Hindoo fakirs.

It is claimed by some that the key to this magical art was lost to Solomon in the death of Hiram Abiff, the widow's son, who was the Grand Master of the Lodge, and since the substitution of the other word the Masons have lost the control over this occult force, by which they were in olden times enabled to work wonders, which are recorded in the Bible and on obelisks and pyramids of Egypt.

It is claimed that Jesus Christ was an adept, and through his knowledge he was enabled to perform so many miracles. To the initiated it was not strange, but it was done in accordance with natural forces and the fixed laws of occultism.

The trident of Paracelsus was believed to have all the virtues the cabala attributes to the words, and which the hierophants of Alexandria ascribed to the celebrated word *Abracadabra*. It gave a complete knowledge and mastery of nature, the secrets of the future, and the command of the elementary spirits; to heal the sick, to move things around with an invisible hand, to call up the spirits of the dead, and do many things that are now done by spiritual mediums. The tipping of tables, raps and independent slate writing were all known to the ancient adepts.

In the books of Moses there are many instances of the magicians performing wonders, and the Egyptian magicians could do what Aaron and Moses did, only Aaron's rod made the biggest snake and gobbled up all the rest; so if it is a snake story, Moses' was the biggest.

These magicians played an important part in the Persian religion, and when the Jews returned from their Babylonian captivity, they brought back with them the secrets of the magician, and they played an important part, and out of them they manufactured their devil, or evil one, with whom they used to scare the ignorant into submission; for they ruled the people and used this art to make them believe it was the work of Jehovah; for all the miracles claimed to be done by them were the same as those performed by the ancient Persian and Egyptian magicians.

Simon Magus could fly off in the air before his disciples and the crowd of witnesses, without going through any circle-making used by the jugglers; nor is this art confined to the ancients. Mr. Turner, the author of the "Embassy to Thibet," tells some strange stories, and he corroborates the story of the Abbe Huc of the reincarnation of Buddha, and that of Lahma (priests) sending their astral souls oft to perform missions and carry messages, what we call mental telegraphy.

The wonderful things done by the magicians of Kashmir, Thibet, Mongolia and Great Tartary are too well known to need comment. If jugglers they be, they have defied all detection even by the best and most expert necromancer of Europe and America. (See Jamblicher's *Mysteries Egypt*, I. 26, Theurgy.)

Epimenides, the Orphikos, was renowned for his sacred and marvelous nature. He had the faculty of sending his soul out of his body as long as he pleased.

Apollonius could at any time send his soul out. He was a great magician.

Empedocles of Agrigenteum, the Pythagorean thaumaturgist, required no conditions to arrest a waterspout which had broken over a city. Neither did he need any to recall a woman to life. He used no dark rooms or cabinets, vanishing suddenly in the air before the eyes of the Emperor Domitian and a whole crowd of witnesses (many thousands). He appeared an hour later in the grotto of Puteoli. He evidently did it by sending off his astral body, while his own physical body he rendered invisible by the concentration of akasa about it, then quietly walked out of the crowd to some retreat, where he remained until the return of his double or astral soul.

The astral soul scin-lecca (double) is able to draw itself out of the body while in a profound sleep, and often travels around and sees places, so that when the person is awake and comes across these places he is sometimes impressed that he has been there before. Some persons' visions are so clear that they are able to see these astral bodies, and it has given rise to spooks and ghosts. Some mediums are able to withdraw their astral hands, and this accounts for an extra hand often witnessed at seances Little by little the whole astral body may ooze out like a passing cloud, until two forms appear where there was only one, the one more shadowy than the other.

The trinity of nature is the lock of magic, the trinity of man the key that fits it It is unthinkable and unpronounceable, and yet every man finds in himself his God "Who "art thou, O fair being?" inquired the disembodied soul in the *Khordah Avesta*, at the gates of Paradise "I am, O Soul, thy good and "purest thoughts, thy works and thy good law, "* * thy angel * * and thy God" Then man or soul is reunited with *itself*, for this "son of God" is one with him, it is his own mediator, the God of his human soul and his justifier "God not revealing himself immediately to man, the spirit is his interpreter," says Plato in the Banquet

Paracelsus says, "The human spirit is so "great a thing that no man can express it! "As God himself is eternal and unchangeable, "so also is the mind of man If we rightly "understood its powers nothing would be im- "possible to us on earth The imagination is "strengthened and developed through faith in "our will. Faith must confirm the imagina- "tion, for faith establishes the will."

Jacolliot, the great writer and translator of Oriental literature, says that "it is impossible "for him to give an account of the marvelous "facts witnessed while among the Hindoos. "The many strange and startling things done by "them would, if told, tend to make the Euro- "peans look upon me as a Munchausen, or a "greater liar than Sinbad the Sailor." But adds with entire truthfulness, "Let it suffice to' "say, that in regard to magnetism and spiritism "Europe has yet to stammer over the first let- "ters of the alphabet, and that the Brahmans "have reached, in these two departments of "learning, results in the way of phenomena, "that are truly stupefying When one sees "these strange manifestations, whose power one "cannot deny, without grasping the laws that "the Brahmans keep so carefully concealed, the "mind is overwhelmed with wonder and lost in "amazement.

"The only explanation we have been able to "obtain on the subject from a learned Brahman "with whom we were on terms of the closest "intimacy was this. ' You have studied phys- "ical nature, and you have obtained, through "the laws of nature, marvelous results—steam, "electricity, etc For twenty thousand years "or more we have studied the intellectual "forces; we have discovered their laws, and we "obtain, by making them act alone or in con- "cert with other matter, phenomena still more "astonishing than your own

"While there are in the science which the "Brahmans call occult, phenomena so extraor- "dinary as to baffle all investigation, there is "not one which cannot be explained, and "which is not subject to natural law, if prop- "erly understood, which any initiated Brahman "could if he would explain every phenomena, "while our ablest physicist is not able to explain "even the most trivial occult phenomenon "produced by a fakir pupil of a pagoda, much "less those performed by an adept "

To comprehend the principles of the natural law involved in occultism, we must keep in mind the fundamental proposition of Oriental philosophy 1. There is no miracle Every- thing that happens is the result of law—eternal, immutable, ever active (Apparent miracle is but the operation of forces antagonistic to the well-ascertained laws of nature, but are un- known to science) And what is not known or understood has always been considered by the ignorant as a miracle

2. Nature is triune There is a visible, objec- tive nature, an invisible, indwelling, energizing nature, the external model of the other, and its vital principle; and above these two, *spirit*, source of all forces, alone eternal and inde- structible The lower two, consequently, change, the highest, the third, does not

3 Man is also triune. He has his physical body; his vitalizing, astral or spiritual body,

the real man; and these two are brooded over and illuminated by the third—the sovereign, the *immortal soul*. When the real man succeeds in merging himself with the latter, he becomes an immortal entity.

4. Magic, as a science, is a knowledge of these principles, and of the way by which the omniscience and omnipotence of the spirit and its control over nature's forces may be acquired by the individual while still in the body. Magic, as an art, is the application of this knowledge in practice.

5. Arcane knowledge misapplied is sorcery; beneficially used, true magic or wisdom.

6. Mediumship is the opposite of adeptship. The medium is the passive instrument of foreign influences; the adept actively controls himself and all inferior potencies.

7. All things that ever were, that now are or shall be, having their record upon the astral light, or tablet of the unseen universe, the initiated adept, by using the vision of his own spirit, can know all that has known or can be known.

8. Races of men differ in spiritual gifts, as in color, stature, or any other external quality. Among some peoples seership naturally prevails. among others, mediumship. Some are addicted to sorcery, and transmit its secret rules of practice from generation to generation, with a range of psychical phenomena, more or less wide, as the result.

9. One phase of magical skill is the voluntary and conscious withdrawal of the inner man (astral form) from the outer man (physical body). In the cases of some mediums withdrawal occurs, but it is unconscious and involuntary. With the latter the body is more or less cataleptic at such times; but with the adept the absence of the astral form would not be noticed, for the physical senses are alert, and the individual appears only as though in a fit of abstraction, " a brown study," as some call it.

The astral form can go anywhere, penetrate any obstacle, neither time nor space are to be considered; it moves with the rapidity of thought and the wings of electricity. The thaumaturgist skilled in the occult science, can make his astral form visible, and assume protean shapes and appear at different places, and by his will-power can cast a mesmeric hallucination over

his audience so as to make them believe that what they saw was real, when in reality it was but a picture in their minds, so impressed by him; while his physical body seems to disappear or assume any shape that he may choose. In this way he quietly slips away and leaves his astral body, then this astral form suddenly rises and floats off in the air, which the spectators mistook for the real body.

Swedenborgians believe, and arcane science teaches, that the soul often leaves and abandons the body, from various causes, as that of overpowering grief, fright, despair, violent attack of sickness, or excessive sensuality, and leaves the vacant carcass, which may be entered and inhabited by the astral form of an adept sorcerer or an elementary (an earth-bound disembodied human soul). In cases of insanity the patient's astral being is either semi-paralyzed, bewildered and subject to the influence of every passing spirit of any sort, or it has departed from the body forever, and the body is taken possession of by some vampyrish entity near its own disintegration and clinging desperately to earth, whose sensual pleasures it may enjoy and prolong for awhile.

Magic is the knowledge of magnetism and electricity, their qualities, correlations and potencies, and their effects on the animal kingdom and man. It is essential wisdom, nature, the material ally, pupil and servant of the magician. As one common vital principle pervades all things, and this is controllable by the perfected human will, the adept by the knowledge of its laws can stimulate the movement of the material forces in plants and animals in a preternatural degree, by using and controlling these hidden forces in nature to quicken the conditions of its nature, and produce more rapid results; thus, for example, make a plant mature in a few minutes which would take months and years by the slow natural growth. Many minerals and plants have within them hidden powers, such as lodestone, opium and hasheesh. The adept can control the sensitive and alter the conditions of the physical and astral bodies of other persons not adepts. He can also govern and employ as he pleases the spirits of the elements, but not that of immortal spirit.

There are two kinds of seership—that of the

soul and that of the spirit. The seership of the ancient Pythoness, or of the modern mesmerized subject, vary but in the artificial modes adopted to induce the state of clairvoyance. But as the vision of both depends upon the acuteness of the senses of the astral body, they differ very widely from the perfect, omniscient spiritual state; for at best the subject can get but glimpses of truth through the veil which physical nature interposes.

The astral principle or mind, called by the Hindu *Yogin Flav-atma*, is the sentient soul, inseparable from our physical brain, which it holds in subjection, and is in its turn equally trammeled by it. This is the *ego*, the intellectual life-principle of man, his conscious entity. While yet in the material body the correctness of its spiritual vision depends on its more or less intimate relation to its higher principle. When the relation is such as to allow the most ethereal portions of the soul-essence to act independently of its grosser particles and of the brain, it can unerringly comprehend what it sees, then only is it the pure, rational, supersentient soul. That state is known in India as the *samaddi*; it is the highest spiritual condition known to man.

But when the body is in a total catalepsy of the physical frame, the soul of the clairvoyant may liberate itself and perceive things subjectively; and yet, as the sentient principle of the brain is alive and active, these pictures of the past, present and future, will be tinctured with the terrestrial perceptions of the objective world; the physical memory and fancy will be in the way of clear vision. But the seer adept knows how to suspend the mechanical action of the brain, by forcing to stop thinking. His vision will be clear as truth itself, uncolored and undistorted; whereas the clairvoyant, unable to control the vibrations of the astral waves, will perceive, more or less, but broken images through the medium of the brain. The seer can never take fleeting shadows for realities, for his memory being as completely subjected to his will as the rest of the body, he receives impressions directly from his spirit. Between his subjective and objective selves there are no obstructive mediums. This is the real spiritual seership in which, according to an expression of Plato, soul is raised above all inferior good.

When we reach "that which is supreme, which is *simple, pure and unchangeable, without form, color or human qualities,* the God—*our nous.*" This is the state which such seers as Plotinus and Appollonius termed "union to the Deity," which the ancient Yogins called *Isvara* and the modern call *Samaddi.* But this state is as far above modern clairvoyance as the stars above the glow-worm. Plotinus, as is well known, was a clairvoyant-seer during his whole life, and yet he had been united to his God but six times during his life, as he confessed to Porphyry.

The Brahmans divide these powers into eight degrees or powers: 1, Anima; 2, Mahima; 3, Layhima; 4, Garima; 5, Prapi; 6, Prakamga; 7, Vasitwa; 8, Isitwa, or divine power. The fifth predicting future events, understanding unknown languages, curing diseases, divining unexpressed thoughts, understanding the language of the heart. The sixth is the power of converting old age into youth. The seventh is the power of mesmerizing human beings and beasts and making them obedient; it is the power of resisting passions and emotions. The eighth power is the spiritual state, and presupposes the absence of the above seven powers, as in this state the Yogi is full of God.

Subjective communication with the human, god-like spirits of those who have preceded us to the silent land of bliss, is in India divided into three categories. Under the spiritual training of a Guru or Lanrizasi the vaton (disciple or neophyte) begins to feel them. Were he not, under the immediate guidance of an adept, he would be controlled by the invisibles, and utterly at their mercy, for among these subjective influences he is unable to discern the good from the bad. Happy the sensitive who is sure of the purity of his spiritual atmosphere.

To this subjective consciousness, which is the *first degree* is after a time added that of clairaudience. This is the second degree or stage of development. The sensitive—when not naturally made so by psychological training—now audibly hears but is still unable to discern, and is incapable of verifying his impressions, and one who is unprotected the tricky powers of the air but too often delude with semblances of voices and speech. But the Guru's influence is there; it is the most powerful shield against the intrusions of the Chritwa into the atmosphere of the vaton, consecrated to the pure, human and celestial Pitris.

When a Buddhist ascetic has reached the fourth degree, he is considered a rahat. He produces every kind of phenomena by the soul power of his freed spirit. A rahat, says the Buddhist, is one who has acquired the power of flying in the air, becoming invisible, commanding the elements, and working all manner of wonders, commonly, but erroneously, called (*meipo*) miracles. He is a perfect man, a demigod. A god he will become when he reaches *Nervana*, for, like the initiates of both testaments, the worshipers of Buddha know that they "are gods."

The astral soul has only passed from the visible to the invisible world, and may be perceived by the inner sense of vision, which is adapted to the things of that other and more real universe. The same rule applies to sound, as the physical ear discerns the vibrations of the atmosphere up to a certain point, not yet definitely fixed, but varying with the individual, so the adept whose interior hearing has been developed, can take the sound at this vanishing point and hear its vibrations in the astral light indefinitely. He needs no wires, helices or sounding-boards; his will-power is all-sufficient. Hearing with spirit, time and distance offer no impediments, and so he may converse with another adept at the antipodes with as great ease as though they were in the same room.

Spiritual Life is the primordial principle above Physical Life, it is the primordial principle behind; but they are one under their dual aspect. "As it is above, so it is below; as in heaven, so on earth." One is the counterpart of the other; one is spiritual, and the other is material or terrestrial.

Magic, in ancient times, was considered as a divine science; wisdom and knowledge of God. The healing art in the temples of Æsculapius, and at the shrines of Egypt and the East, was always magical, and the secrets intrusted only to the initiated. Then the priest was the medical adviser of soul and body, as the former has much to do with the latter, as it is conceded that the mind has much influence over the body, and health depends on that of a sound mind; therefore to be a successful physician he must understand both body and mind, and the soul

is embraced in the latter, and has control of it, which is immortal and becomes more active after the soul has left the body.

The inner entity of man is more or less divine according to its proximity to the crown—christos. The purer and better a man is, the closer and more serene is his life and freer from external dangers, and the clearer and better are his impressions and his visions into the future. It is this that has, in all ages of the world, convinced man that an immortal spirit exists within him, which under favorable circumstances, can converse with angels, who are nothing but progressed souls that at one time dwelt in a physical body. This is admitted often in the Bible, and by the greatest philosophers of antiquity; and if it could then exist, there is no reason why it cannot now, as the laws of nature never change. These spirits, or guardian angels, have often appeared to man and warned him of danger, and revealed the future to him, by touch, glance or word, as Ammonius tells us. Moreover, Lamprius and others held that if the unembodied spirits, or souls, could descend on earth and become guardians of mortal men, "we should not seek to deprive those souls which are still in the body of that power by which the former know future events and are able to announce them. It is not probable," adds Lamprius, "that the soul gains a new power of prophecy after separation from the body which it did not possess before." We may rather conclude it possessed all these powers during its union with the body, although in a lesser perfection. Like the sun it always shines bright and clear, but its rays are dimmed to us when it passes behind a cloud or is obscured by an eclipse; so it is with the soul when it is confined in the flesh.

Yet some persons are so spiritual that they are able to hold converse with spirits and angels, by which means they are enabled to get a glimpse of the spirit world. Those disembodied spirits that have progressed and learned the laws of the spirit land, are more able to see and tell what the future results will be, as a man is better able to judge the future than an inexperienced boy is; as knowledge of cause and effect will enable one to come at the result, as everything is governed by certain laws, and to understand these laws is only finding out the secrets of nature that will enable man to use them and to advance himself in the search of truth, which is the ultimate end of all research.

Akasa, or Life Force.

It was Ammonius who first taught that every religion was based on one and the same truth, which is the wisdom found in the books of Thoth (Hermese Trismegistus), from which books Pythagoras and Plato had learned all their philosophy, and the doctrines of the former he affirmed to have been identical with the earliest teachings of the Brahmans, now embodied in the old Vedas. "The name Thoth," says Professor Wilder, "means a college or assembly," and it is not improbable that the books were so named as being the collected oracles and doctrines of the sacerdotal fraternity of Memphis. Rabbi Wise had suggested a similar hypothesis in relation to the divine utterances recorded in the Hebrew Scriptures. But the Hindoo writers assert that during the reign of king Kansa Yadus the High Hierophant alone knew how to perform the solemn operation of infusing his own vital and astral soul into the adept chosen by him for his successor, who thus became endowed with a double life.

Mrs. Britten, in her "Ghost Land," gives a strange account how this mystical operation of the adept to transfer his spiritual entity after the death of his body into the youth he loves with all the ardent love of a spiritual parent, and how he used the organism of the boy in sending his astral soul to different places and to do certain things; all of which is startling, and to the uninitiated it sounds like the wildest romance, destitute of truth and in violation of our senses.

"In the remotest ages there has existed a mysterious, awful science, under the name of *Theopœa*. This science taught the art of endowing the various symbols of the gods with temporary life and intelligence. Statues and blocks of inert matter became animated under the potential will of the hierophant. The fire stolen by Prometheus had fallen down in the struggle to earth; it embraced the lower regions of the sky, and settled in the waves of the universal ether, as the potential Akasa of the Hindoo rites. We breathe and imbibe it into our organic system at every inhalation.

But it becomes potential only under the influx of *will and spirit*. Left to itself this life-principle will blindly follow the laws of nature, and, according to conditions, will produce health and exuberance of life, or cause death and dissolution when withdrawn; but guided by the will of the adept, it becomes obedient; its currents restore the equilibrium in organic bodies; they fill the waste and produce physical and psychological miracles well known to mesmerizers. Infused into inorganic and inert matter, they create an appearance of life, hence motion. If to the life an individual intelligence, a personality, is wanting, then the operator must either send his *scin-lecca*, his own astral spirit, to animate it, or use his power over the region of native-spirits to force one of them to infuse his entity into the marble, wood or metal; or again be helped by human spirits.

The good spirits will not infuse their essence into these inanimate objects. They leave it to the lower kinds to produce the similitude of life, animation and materialization. They send their influence through the intervening spheres like a ray of divine light, when the so-called miracle is required for a good purpose. The condition—and this is a law of spiritual nature —is purity of motive, purity of the surrounding magnetic atmosphere, and personal purity of the operator. Thus it is that a pagan miracle may be performad by a fakir of South India. A naked beggar crouched on the floor, with no assistance but his magic power, will so command these hidden forces of nature as to move furniture in the remotest part of the room, even the chair or sofa you may be sitting on; the doors to open or shut, the candle to go out, birds, flames, the forms of men, women and animals to flit before your vision in broad daylight, and many other things too strange and incredible to mention.

The power to move statues and tables is not confined to the ancients, but the nineteenth century is full of such incidents, if we are to believe what man and the papers say. In the summer of 1876, the French papers gave an account of the capers performed by the statue of the Madonna of Lourdes. This gracious lady, says the sexton, has run off into the woods several times, and he was forced to hunt her up and bring her home. After this began a series of miracles, healing, prophesying, letters dropping from on high, and many other strange manifestations. These miracles are implicitly accepted by millions and millions of Catholics, many of them being of the most intelligent and educated classes. Then why should we disbelieve the statements given by the ancient historians? Titus and Livy say that when the statue of Juno was asked if she was willing "to abandon the walls of Veii and change her abode to that of Rome," consented by nodding her head and answering, "Yes, I will." And, says the historian, "Furthermore, upon carrying off the figure, it seemed instantly to lose its *immense weight*," and he adds, "the statue seemed rather to follow than otherwise." (Tite-Livy, v. dec. 1,)

Des Mousseau, a devout Catholic writer, gives many instances of statues of saints and madonnas walking and moving about. He admits that magic can do the same, but that Christianity can beat it; that one is the work of God, while the other is the doings of the devil; and says: "The Holy Roman Catholic and Apostolic Church declares the miracles wrought by the faithful sons are produced by the will of God, and all others the work of the spirits of hell."

The ancients animated statues, and the Hermitists called into being, out of the elements, the shapes of salamanders, gnomes, undines and sylphs, which they did not pretend to create, but simply to make visible by holding open the door of nature, so that under favoring conditions they might step into view. And if the Bible can be taken as authority, "Aaron threw down his rod and it became a serpent. Then Pharaoh also called his wise men and sorcerers; now the magicians of Egypt they did also in like manner, * * and they became serpents, but Aaron's rod swallowed up their rods," Aaron by a wave of his rod brought forth frogs, and the magicians did the same; so that the magicians could do almost all things that Aaron did: yet Aaron could excel, and Pharaoh concluded that the best thing he could do was to let the children of Israel go.

Now these manifestations of power do not exceed what the magicians and fakirs claim to do and have often done in the presence of the most reliable and skillful scientific Europeans, and they have been unable to detect any fraud or delusion; so it is reasonable to suppose that if the ancient magicians of Egypt could perform these wonderful feats, they could be done now under favorable circumstances, and that this secret is claimed by the Hindoos to be the same art that has been known in India for thousands of years.

The Hindoo adepts claim to possess the power of controlling the akasa (or life-principle), by means of which they are able to kill a person and bring him to life, by directing a current of this akasa upon the wound and healing it.

The performance of the fakirs are wonderful and defy all detection of trickery. They have been known to be buried alive and grain sown upon the grave, and in thirty days were dug up alive. They will inflict mortal wounds and exhibit their bowels to persons present, and then heal the wounds immediately. Some of these fakirs exhibited their marvelous power to the Prince of Wales when in India. One of the fakirs gave one of his company a vessel to hold; it soon turned to a cobra, a most poisonous serpent, and it was examined and found to be alive and had fangs. If it had bitten any one, it would have been instant death. They gave some mango seed to the prince to be selected by him. It was then placed in a pot of earth; in a few moments it came up, put forth leaves, buds and blossoms, and in about four minutes matured fruit that was pronounced by all present to be a fresh mango.

The same thing was done in the presence of Dr. J. M. Peebles, in the open air; of which he gives an account, during his travels in India. Almost any traveler in that country will corroborate this statement.

Wonder-Workers of India.

Fakirs can be buried for months, as has been testified by English officers—Lord Napier, Captain Osborne and Sir Claude Wade. Captain Osborne says he "saw one of the fakirs buried for six weeks beneath my floor, and to prevent any chance of deception a guard of four soldiers was detailed to watch day and night to see there was no deception." "On opening it," says Sir Claude, "we saw a figure enclosed in a bag of white linen fastened by a string over the head. * * * The servant then began pouring warm water over the figure. * * *

. The legs and arms of the body were shriveled and stiff, the face full, the head resting on the shoulders like a corpse. I then called the medical man who was attending me to come down and inspect the body, which he did but could discover no pulsation in the heart, the temples or the arms. There was, however, a heat about the region of the brain, but no other part of the body exhibited any. The body was then taken and placed in a warm bath, friction was applied, the removal of wax, and cotton pledgets from the nostrils and ears, the rubbing of the eyelids with ghee and clarified honey. Then they applied a hot cohesive cake of bread to the top of his head. After three applications of the hot cake to his head, the body was convulsed, the nostrils inflated and respiration begun, the limbs assumed a natural fullness, the pulsation was only perceptible. The tongue was anointed with ghee, and unrolled where the end had been placed in the gullet to prevent any air entering the stomach, the eyeballs became dilated and recovered their natural color, and the fakir recognized those present and spoke."

This plugging up process was done to keep the air from entering upon the organic tissues of the body and prevented decomposition, so that he was hermetically sealed up Now if the fakirs can suspend life in this way and then restore animation, why should not we give credence to the fact as stated of Jesus Christ resurrecting Lazarus? and that of Appolonius who restored to life a girl? and that one mentioned by Diogenes Laertius restored to life by Empedocles? Yet these were pagans and are discarded, while that of Christ is alone believed to be true The prodigies of Jesus and Appolonius are so well attested that they appear authentic Whether in either or both cases life was simply suspended or not, the important fact remains that by some power peculiar to themselves, both the wonder-workers recalled the seemingly dead to life in an instant. The books are full of instances where people have been buried or nearly committed to the tomb who were only in a cataleptic state.

The many strange stories told by travelers in the East would fill volumes. One given to a delegation of the East India Company is thus related : " A lot of Englishmen who visited the Indian prince Jehangire, saw two tents erected about a bow-shot apart. Then the fakir asked the guests what kind of animals they wished to see fight ? One said, ' Ostriches.' At a signal given out stalked a couple of those birds, one from each tent which they had seen erected with nothing in them ; they fought some time, the blood ran down their necks where they had bitten each other. They returned, at a given word, to the tents. Then another of the company called for a lion fight. Out of each tent walked a lion ; after rolling over and biting one another, roaring and tearing up the ground, they retired at a given word Then out came two wild buffaloes, and they had a pitched battle. All this was done in the presence of the whole court. These Bengalese conjurers and jugglers then took ten mulberry seeds, which they planted in the earth. In a few minutes they produced ten trees. The ground parted, the sprouts came up, pushing out leaves, twigs and branches, spreading wide out in the air, budding, blossoming and yielding fruit which matured on the spot, which they tasted and pronounced good. Figs, almond, mango and walnut were planted ; they likewise grew up rapidly before their eyes The branches of these trees were filled with birds of the richest plumage, flitting among the leaves and singing sweet notes. The leaves then turned russet, fell off, branches and twigs withered, and finally the trunks sank back into the earth. If all transpired in less than an hour

" A large cauldron was then produced, and a quantity of rice was thrown into it. Without the least sign of fire it began to boil; and out of this cauldron were taken hundreds of plates of cooked rice, with a stewed fowl on the top of each." This trick is performed on a smaller scale by the most ordinary fakirs of the present day in India. This was equal to that of Christ feeding the multitude on a few loaves and fishes.

In the memoirs of the emperor Jehangire (page 99), there is a strange account given by an eye-witness : " The performance of the seven jugglers of Bengal. They took a man and chopped each limb off and severed his head from the body. They scattered the mutilated members around on the ground for some time; they then threw a sheet over them, and one of the jugglers crept under it. In a few moments he came out, followed by the mutilated man that a few moments before had been cut all to pieces. They then took a chain," says the writer, "some fifty cubits long, and threw one end up until it went out of sight, and then it remained suspended in the air. A dog was then produced, placed at the lower end of the chain, when he ran up it out of sight. Next was a hog, a lion and a tiger, all did the same thing."

Another account of a fakir, given in the *Franco-American*, is ahead of this: "He took a peg and drove into the ground, threw up a ball with a cord attached, which went out of sight; he then sent up a boy, and as he did not return he said he would go after him. Soon down came a hand of the boy, then a leg, then the body all bloody, then came the head; presently down came the juggler with a bloody knife in his hand. He picked up the different parts of the boy and threw them into a basket, when out jumped the boy and ran off."

They are known to plant the hilts of their sharp swords in the ground, then lay down on the points, while one by one these swords were removed until he lay in the air without any support; and an Englishman says he took a stick and felt under the body and could find no support. Says Colonel Yule: "They will stick a live pig to a rock so it can't get away, restore the dead to life, catch wild beasts with their hands, read thoughts, make water flow backward, eat tiles, sit in the midair, etc." An old legend ascribed to Simon Magus precisely the same power: "He made statues to walk, leaped into the fire without being burned, flew in the air, made bread of stones, changed his shape, assumed two faces at once, converted himself into a pillar, caused doors to open at will," etc.

Origen writes that the Brahmans always were famous for their wonderful cures, which they performed by the utterance of certain words; and the present travelers in India say it is still practiced, and that upon pronouncing a certain word or sentence they are able to perform wonderful tricks. Some will walk barefooted on red, burning coals, on the points of sharp knives stuck in the ground, stand posed on the big toe on the point of one of them, and lift up another man from off the ground. I have seen a Japanese juggler do the same, ascend a ladder bare-footed the rounds of which were very sharp

swords. I have also seen an East India negro, called the "Fire King," walk on hot bars of iron, take and bend them under his foot and up around his leg; the outer skin would smoke and fry a little, but it did not produce apparently any pain. He took his finger and stirred up a ladle of molten lead, then took a table-spoonful of the melted lead and put it into his mouth, and then spat it out on the floor, which I undertook to pick up but got my fingers burned. He also took a dish of alcohol, put a lot of tow in it, stirred it up and set it on fire, took a fork and began to eat it, the blaze rising up over his head. After chewing it awhile, the fire blazing out whenever he opened his mouth, then spitting it out on the floor it burned the wood. He blew the flames out of his mouth on my hand, and it burned it and singed the hair. All of this was done in broad daylight, within a few feet of myself and hundreds of others. He would stick his hands into the furnace, take up a coal of fire and light his pipe. I examined his hands and feet; there appeared to be no foreign substance on them, but the outer skin appeared a little parched and discolored. There was no one present who did not believe that what he did was genuine, as several like myself got their fingers burned in testing it. He said that he would not mind to walk into the hottest furnaces, like that spoken of in the Bible where the Hebrew children walked through the fiery furnace, and from appearances he might have done it.

In Siam, Japan and Great Tartary, it is the custom to make medallions, statuets and idols out of the ashes of cremated persons. They are mixed with water into a paste, and after being molded into any desired shape, are baked and then gilded and kept as household gods. The cremation is done to facilitate the withdrawal of the astral soul, which lingers more or less until the bones are decomposed, and therefore they cremate the bodies of their departed friends, and fearing that the astral soul might remain satisfied for an indefinite period within the ashes, they resort to the following process: "The sacred dust is placed in a heap upon a metallic plate strongly magnetized, of the size of a man's body. The adept then slowly and gently fans it with a peculiar fan, and at the same time making signs and muttering a form of invocation. The ashes then begin to move and assume the outlines of the body before cremation. Then there gradually arises a sort of whitish vapor, which after a time forms into an erect column, and compacting itself is finally transformed into the 'double' or ethereal astral counterpart of the dead, which in its turn dissolves away into the air and disappears from mortal sight." This accounts for the Hindoos preferring cremation, as it sets the astral body free from the earthly remains, around which it lingers until it dissolves back into its original elements.

This wonderful power has existed in all ages of the world in some phase or other, to illuminate dark and benighted man, to elevate him and cause him to look up to a higher and better life to come. History, sacred and profane, is full of it. Whether it came from natural-born mediums, or learned by association with those versed in the occult sciences of the Oriental world, where it has been known from time immemorial and sacredly guarded by the Brahmans, Buddhists, fakirs, the ancient Egyptians, heliophants, with whom Moses learned the art and introduced it among the Jews under the Order of the Kabalist, and out of which Freemasonry has sprung, as Solomon sent his ships to Ophir for gold and frankincense, myrrh and pea-feathers, which land was no doubt India.

In India, Malabar, and some places in Central Africa, the conjurers will let a person fire his own musket or revolver at them without ever touching or interfering in loading it Laing, in his travels, gives an instance of it. Salvert gives a similar instance in his Philosophy of Occult Sciences. In 1568 the Prince of Orange condemned a Spanish prisoner to be shot at Juliers The soldier was tied to a tree and shot at by a file of soldiers, but the balls took no effect. It was supposed that he had a coat of armor on; he was stripped; they found he only had an amulet on, which was taken off Then he was fired at and fell dead. Not many years ago there lived in Abyssinia a sorcerer who would let the European travelers fire at him with their own guns loaded by them with their own balls, for a trifle. At last they offered him five francs to let them place the muzzle of the gun next to the body. After consulting the

spirits by placing his ear to the ground, he consented The gun bursted and the conjurer was unhurt. An Indian said that Washington was not to be killed by a bullet, as he had fired at him seventeen times within short range without ever touching him at Braddock's defeat; and it is remarkable that he never was wounded during the whole of his life, yet he was often in the thickest of the fight In fact many great generals have been believed by their soldiers to have a "charmed life" Prince Emile von Sayne-Wittgenstein, of the Russian army, is said to be one possessed of a charmed life

There are persons who have the power to psychologize birds and kill them by will power. Jacques Pelessier, in the province of Le Var, France, in 1864, made his living by catching and killing birds by his will power, which was thoroughly tested by men of science Fourteen birds were taken in this way in one hour, none could resist his power By stretching out his hand towards them they became powerless. It at once put them into a cataleptic sleep, and the phenomena proved to be a magnetic action. But his power was confined to sparrows, robins, goldfinches and meadow larks, and he could not charm other birds

There are persons in India and Africa that can charm snakes, crocodiles, and wild animals like the tiger, which have been known to go up and lick the hands of a fakir when asleep in the jungles, and not injure him.

The Buddhists claim that the spirit of Buddha becomes reincarnated in the flesh after death, so that he ever lives, passing from out the old body at death and entering into that of a young child. The scene of the reincarnation is given by a Florentine scientist, who visited Thibet in the early part of this century, having been permitted to penetrate in disguise to the hallowed precincts of a Buddhist temple, where the most solemn of all ceremonies takes place, which are shut out from the gaze of the uninitiated. "An altar is ready in the temple to receive the resuscitated Buddha found by the initiated priesthood, and recognized by certain secret signs to have reincarnated himself in a new-born infant. The baby, but a few days old, is brought into the presence of the people and reverentially placed upon the altar. Suddenly rising into a sitting posture, the child begins to utter, in a loud, manly voice, the following sentences ' I am Buddha; I am his spirit, and I, Buddha, your Dolai Lama, have left my old decrepid body, at the temple of * * * and selected the body of this young babe as my next earthly dwelling." He says he was permitted by the priests to take the baby in his arms and carry it off some distance, so as to satisfy himself that it was no trick of the ventriloquist. The infant opened his eyes and gave him such a look that it made his flesh creep, and repeated the same words, so there could be no mistake about it.

This account is confirmed by Abbe Huc, a celebrated Catholic priest who traveled through this country, and he further states that the child answers questions and tells those who knew him in " his past life the most exact details of his anterior earthly existence." But he was unfrocked by the church because he was sincere and stuck to the truth of the assertion

But this is not the only instance of babies speaking Jacques Dubois gives an account of the Camissard prophets in 1707, among whom was a boy fifteen months old, who spoke in good French " as though God were speaking through his mouth;" and there are the Cevennes babies whose speaking and prophesying were witnessed by the first savans of France, which has passed into history uncontradicted. Lloyd's *Weekly Newspaper* for March, 1875, contains an account of the following phenomena: " At Saar-Louis, France, a child was born; the mother had just been delivered, and the midwife was holding the child in her hands, when some one asked what was the hour. To the astonishment of all present the new-born babe replied distinctly, ' Two o'clock.' While they all were looking at the infant in speechless wonder and dismay, it opened its eyes and said: ' I have been sent into the world to tell you that 1875 will be a good year, but that 1876 will be a year of blood.' Having uttered this prophecy it turned on its side and expired, aged half an hour." The truth of this prophecy is too late to admit of a comment, as 1875 was a year of great plenty, and 1876 one of bloody scenes on the Danube, between the Turks and Russians, unparalleled except in the butchery of the Indians in North and South America, and the wading in blood of the English to the throne of Delhi.

There are many instances of the precocity of children, but I will only relate one more, that of a child of H. D. Jencken, M. R. I , barrister at law, London, whose mother was the famous Kate Fox, of Rochester rapping notoriety. When the child was only three months old, it showed evidence of mediumship by raps on the pillow and cradle, and when five months old wrote a communication of twenty words.

PROPHECY can only be explained by spirits impressing the person, as spirits of higher intelligence are able to combine causes and effects and can tell more readily what the result will be than a man; so can a man foretell events better than a child, and in this obscure way certain persons in a peculiar state may have visions and get a glimpse into the future. But spirits, like men, are limited in their knowledge, and some know more than others; so it depends on the source and the knowledge of the spirit. The Bible and history are full of prophecy. Much of it has been fulfilled, and much of it has not. Governor Talmadge gives an account of how a distinguished citizen's life was saved on board of the United States war ship Princeton, by a premonition. Rev. Dr. Wilson, of Allegheny City, prophecied the great fire of 1845 in Pittsburg, the Mexican war and its results, the war between Russia and the Western powers, and the speedy limitation of the temporal power of the Pope.

Napoleon, while an exile on the island of St. Helena, made the following prediction about the United States: " Ere the close of the nineteenth century, America will be convulsed with one of the greatest revolutions the world has ever witnessed Should it succeed, her power and prestige are lost; but should the Government maintain her supremacy, she will be on a firmer basis than ever. The theory of a republican form of government will be established, and she will defy the world " History gives us prophecies of Hannibal and Napoleon, which were fulfilled. Whether old Mother Shipley's prophecy will come true remains to be seen; yet much of it has come to pass, but the world did not end in 1882.

How the spirits arrive at these facts is unknown; yet they may, like the astronomer who by calculation is able to tell when an eclipse of the sun or moon will take place for hundreds of years to come. To the ignorant this appears to be impossible. The truth of science, of all knowledge, is to afford facilities to predict the unknown, and judge the future by the past —the cause and effect—will produce certain results if their relation is properly understood. But there is much depending on the environments, and these are forever changing, so that it is impossible for even the most advanced minds to see all that may happen or change the course of things and events. So long as knowledge is limited, so long will prophecies prove failures.

Destiny.

"Man, therefore, to a certain extent, is a being of destiny, which is ever weaving thread by thread around himself, as a spider does his cobweb; and this destiny is guided either by that presence termed by some the guardian angel, or more intimate astral inner man, who is too often the evil genius of the man of flesh. But these lead on the outward man, but one of them must prevail, and from the very beginning of the invisible affray the stern implacable *law of compensation* steps in and takes its course, following faithfully the fluctuations. When the last strand is woven, and man is seemingly enwrapped in the network of his own doing,˙then he finds himself completely under the empire of his *self-made* destiny. It then either fixes him like the inert shell of an oyster against the immovable rock, or like a feather carries him away in a whirlwind raised by his own actions."

An Occult Fraternity.

"There is an occult fraternity which has existed from very ancient times, having a hierarchy of officers, secret signs and passwords, and a peculiar method of instruction in science, religion and philosophy. If we may believe those who at present profess to belong to it, the philosopher's stone, the elixir of life, the art of invisibility, and the power of communicating directly with the ultra-mundane life, are a part of the inheritance they possess." These adepts are of a limited number, seldom remain long in any place, but leave without creating notice. They all appear to be men from forty to fifty years old, possessed of vast erudition, and can speak in many tongues. They are men of mod-

erate means, caring little for wealth, yet always have enough to supply their wants. They live pure and blameless lives, are austere in manners and almost ascetic in their habits.

There is a mystical fraternity now established in the United States, which claims an intimate relationship with one of the oldest and most powerful of Eastern Brotherhoods. It is known as the Brotherhood of Luxor. It has many faithful members widely scattered throughout the West. They have many important secrets of science which they guard with great jealousy, but which they are willing to impart to man when he has advanced enough to receive them. No one can become a member unless he be a person endowed with certain intellectual gifts by birth. No position, rank or money can procure a membership. Nature places the stamp by which they are recognized. Its officers and records are kept in the spirit world, who impart to the initiate whatever knowledge they see proper to confer. They never mistake a person nor his fidelity to keep a secret.

We have a very interesting account of one of these adepts in the strange and interesting work of Emma Harding Britten, "The Ghost Land or Occultism," who, she says, wrote the "ART MAGI," which she had published; and if the statement therein made be true, it is stranger than fiction, and well may one exclaim in the language of Hamlet: "There are more things in heaven and earth, Horatio, than are dreamed of in your philosophy."

These adepts hold their conclaves in an enchanted cave in India, where invisible spirits reveal themselves to the adept and mingle together in the human form. They perform wonders that no mortal can understand. They introduce the adept by passing through underground passages, where rocks part to admit their ingress and egress. The cavern is lit up by a luminous light that radiates from their heads; the walls reflect this light like thousands of diamonds and crystals. The spirits flit hither and thither. The brain of the adept becomes bewildered, and in a semi-conscious state he is led forth to the light of day, not knowing whence he came.

Madame Blavatsky, Secretary of the Theosophical Society and author of " Isis Unvailed," has made wonderful progress in the occult sciences, so that she has been able to send messages to the adepts of Kashmir valley, hundreds of miles off, and receive answers without any visible means. The messages come, and are placed wherever she requests. At her command the invisible power takes it and soon returns with the answer from some of the Yhebian brothers. Wherever she goes there are persons impressed to meet her with conveyance or money. She has traveled over India in company with Alcott, another adept.

"The keys to the biblical miracles of old, and to the phenomena of modern days; the problems of psychology, physiology, and the many 'missing links' which have so perplexed scientists of late, are all in the hands of secret fraternities. This mystery must be unvailed some day. But till then dark skepticism will constantly interpose its threatening, ugly shadow between God's truths and the spiritual vision of mankind; and many are those who, infected by the moral epidemic of our century—hopeless materialism—will remain in doubt and mortal agony as to whether when man dies he will live again, although the question has been solved by long bygone generations of sages. The answers are there. They may be found in the time-worn granite pages of caves, temples, on sphinxes, propylons and obelisks. They have stood there for untold ages, and neither the rude assault of time, nor the still ruder assault of the hands of the religious fanatic, have succeeded in obliterating the records—all covered with the problems which were solved—who can tell? perhaps by the archaic forefathers of their builders. The solution follows each question, and this the Christian could not appropriate, for except the initiates no one has understood the mystic writings. The key was in the keeping of those who knew how to commune with the invisible Presence, and who had received, from the lips of Mother Nature herself, her grand truths. And so stands these monuments, like mute forgotten sentinels on the threshold of that *unseen* world, whose gates are thrown open but to a few elect. Defying the hand of time, the vain inquiry of profane science, the insults of *revealed* religion, they will disclose their riddles to none but the legatees of those by whom they were intrusted with the MYSTERY. The cold stony lips of the once vocal Memnon, and these hardy sphinxes, keep their secrets well. Who will unseal them? Who of you modern materialistic dwarfs and unbelieving sadducees will dare to lift the VAIL OF ISIS?"

CHAPTER III.

SOUL OF THE UNIVERSE
(ANIMA MUNDI)

Ether—Psychomacy—Plato and St. Paul on the Triune, Body, Spirit and Soul—Transmigration—
Hindoo Idea of a Soul, its Origin and Destiny

The soul of the universe, the great magnetic agent which gives life to all things, is what Sir Isaac Newton calls the *Divine Sensorum*. It is, he says, "a very subtle spirit which penetrates through all things, even the hardest bodies, and is concealed in their substance Through the strength and activity of this spirit bodies attract each other and adhere together when brought into contact. Through it electrical bodies operate at the remotest distance as well as near at hand, attracting and repelling Through this spirit the light also flows, and is refracted and reflected and warms bodies All senses are excited by this spirit, and through it the animals move their limbs But these things cannot be explained in a few words, and we have not yet sufficient experience to determine fully the laws by which this universal spirit operates "

It is an independent life-force that actuates and moves all things The ancient oracles asserted that it was "ether that gave impressions of thoughts, characters and divine visions to men, by which they were able to read the past and the future; that this ether abounded throughout space in which all intelligence was registered, and that the future existed in this astral light in embryo, as the present existed in embryo in the past. While man is free to act as he pleases, the manner in which he *will* act was foreknown from all time, not on the ground of fatalism or destiny, but simply on the principle of universal, unchangeable harmony, and as it may be foreknown that, when a musical note is struck, its vibration will not and cannot change into those of another note Besides that, eternity can have neither past nor future, but only the present, as boundless space, in its strictly literal sense, can have neither distant nor proximate places, as there is no beginning and no end, so that we only catch the reflection of the past and a glimpse of the future Professor Hitchcock says "The human spirit, being of the Divine immortal spirit, appreciates neither past nor future, but sees all things as in the present "

Professor J. W Draper says: "A shadow never falls upon a wall without leaving thereupon a permanent trace, a trace which might be made visible by applying the proper process * * * The portraits of our friends, or landscape views, may be hidden upon the sensitive surface from the eye, but they are ready to make their appearance as soon as a proper developer is resorted to. A specter is concealed on a silver or glassy surface, until by our necromancy we make it come forth into the visible world Upon the walls of our most private apartments, where we think the eye of intrusion is altogether shut out, and our retirement can never be profaned, there exist the vestiges of all our acts, silhouettes of what we have done," so that every thought, act and deed is registered to condemn or justify us when the mind is quickened in death, as is illustrated in the case of a drowning man, when all the long-forgotten scenes of his moral life flash across his memory.

And it is a well-known fact that we often recognize familiar places, landscapes and faces that we have no recollection of ever having seen before This is accounted for on the theory that the spirit has, in its wanderings while the body was wrapped in slumber, seen these faces and places. This gave rise to the idea of transmigration, that the soul had previously been in the body of some one else; and this psychological phenomena is one of the strongest arguments in favor of the immortality of the soul. As Eliphas Levi beautifully expresses it, "Nature shuts the door after everything that passes, and pushes life onward in more perfected forms." The chrysalis becomes a butterfly; but the latter never becomes a grub again.

In the stillness of the night hours, when our bodily senses are fast locked in the fetters of sleep, and our physical body rests, the astral form becomes free. It then oozes out of its earthly prison, and, as Paracelsus has it, "confabulates with the outward world," and "travels round the visible as well as the invisible worlds."

In sleep, he says, "the astral body (soul) is in freer motion; then it roams to its parents and holds converse with the stars. * * * The more the body is exhausted the freer is the spiritual man, and the more vivid the impressions of our soul's memory." Dreams, forebodings, prognostications and presentiments are impressions left by our astral spirit on our brain, which receives them more or less distinctly according to the proportion of blood with which it is supplied during the hours of sleep.

Heavy and robust persons, whose sleep is dreamless and uninterrupted, upon awaking toward consciousness, may' sometimes remember nothing; but impressions of scenes and landscapes which the astral body saw in its peregrinations are still there, though lying latent under the pressure of matter. They may be awakened at any moment, and then, during such flashes of man's inner memory, there is an instantaneous interchange of energies between the visible and the invisible universes. Between the "micrographs" of the cerebral ganglion and the photo-scenographic galleries of the spirit a current is established. Like the audophone of Edison, it only needs the current established, and the words come forth through it. They may have been spoken years before and stored up.

Blumenbach assures us that "in the state of sleep all intercourse between mind and body is suspended." "No man, however gross and material he may be, can avoid leading a double existence—one in the visible universe and the other in the invisible. The *life-principle* which animates his physical frame is chiefly in the spiritual body, and while the mere animal portions of him rest, the more spiritual ones know neither limits nor obstacles. * * * Some might object on the ground taken by theology, that dumb brutes have no immortal souls, and hence can have no spirits. Theologians, as laymen, labor under the erroneous impression that the *soul* and *spirit* are one and the same thing. But if we study Plato and other philosophers of old, we may readily perceive that while the *irrational* soul—by which Plato meant our spiritual body or more ethereal representative of ourselves—can have at best only a prolonged continuity of existence beyond the grave, (which is only the body of the spirit.)

The deeper the trance, the less signs of life the body shows, the clearer become the spiritual perceptions and more powerful is the soul's vision. The soul, disburdened of bodily senses, shows activity of power in a far greater degree of intensity than it can in a strong, healthy body. Brirre de Boismont gives repeated instances of this fact. "The organs of sight, smell, taste, touch and hearing, are proved to become far acuter in a mesmerized subject deprived of the possibility of exercising them bodily, than while he uses them in his normal state." Such facts alone proved, ought to stand as invincible demonstrations of the continuity of individual life, at least for a certain period after the body has been left by us, either by reason of its being worn out or by accident. But during its brief sojourn on earth, our soul may be assimilated to a light hidden under a bushel; it still shines more or less bright, and attracts to itself the influences of kindred spirits, and when a thought, of good or evil import is begotten in our brain, it draws to its impulses of like nature as irresistibly as a magnet attracts iron filings. This attraction is also proportionate to the intensity with which the thought-impulse makes itself felt in the *ether*; and so it will be understood how one man may impress himself upon his own epoch so forcibly that the influence may be carried—through the ever-interchanging currents of the two worlds, the visible and invisible—from one succeeding age to another, until it affects a large portion of mankind.

Regard it as you please, there can be no doubt that the properties of the *ether* are of a much higher order in the arena of nature than those of *tangible matter*, and as even the highest priests of science still find the latter *far beyond* their comprehension, except in numerous but minute and often isolated particles, it would not become us to speculate further. It is sufficient for our purpose to know, from what the ether certainly does, that *it is capable of doing vastly more than any has yet ventured to say.*"

It may be what the Chaldean oracles call ether, for it states that from ether have come all things, and to it all will return; that the images of all things are indelibly impressed upon it, and that it is the storehouse of the germs or of the remains of all visible forms and even ideas.

Psychomancy.

It may be to this subtile force that certain persons, by their sensitive touch against the forehead, are enabled to read names in a folded ballot, or the fragment of an ancient building recall its history and even the scenes which transpired in and about it. A bit of ore will carry the soul's vision back to the time when it was in process of formation. This faculty is called by its discoverer, Professor J. R. Buchanan, of Louisville, Kentucky, *Psychomancy.* He says, "The mental and physiological influence imparted to writing appears to be imperishable. The specimens I have investigated give their impressions with a distinctness and force little impaired by time. Old manuscripts requiring an antiquary to decipher their strange old penmanship, were easily interpreted by the psychometric power. * * * The property of retaining the impress of mind is not limited to writing, drawing, painting. Everything upon which human contact, thought and volition have been expended, may become linked with that thought and life so as to recall them to the mind of another when in contact."

Many tests have been made. A fragment of Cicero's house at Tusculum was given to the psychometer, who placed it to his forehead; he at once described, without the slightest knowledge where the fragment came from, the place and the surrounding of the great orator's home; also, the previous owner of the building, Cornelius Sulla Felix, the dictator, was described. "A fragment of marble from the ancient Christian church of Smyrna brought before the psy-chometer its congregation and its officiating priests. Specimens from Nineveh, China, Jerusalem, Greece, Ararat, and other places all over the world, brought up scenes in life of various personages whose ashes had been scattered thousands of years ago. In many cases Professor Denton verified the statements by reference to historical records. A bit of the skeleton or a fragment of the tooth of some ante-diluvian animal caused the seeress (who was blindfolded) to perceive the creature as it was when alive, and even gave a brief mention of its life and sensations. The psychometer, by applying the fragment of a substance to his forehead, brings his *inner life* into relations with the inner soul of the object he handles."

Professor Denton says: "Not a leaf waves, not an insect crawls, not a ripple moves, but each motion is recorded by a thousand faithful scribes in infallible and indelible scripture. From the dawn of light upon this infant globe, when round its cradle the starry curtains hung, to this moment, nature has been busy photographing everything;" so when the psychometer examines his specimen he is brought into contact with the current of astral light connected with that specimen, and which retains pictures of the event associated with with its history. These, according to Prôfessor Denton, pass before his vision with the swiftness of light, scene after scene crowding upon each other so rapidly that it is only by the superior exercise of will that he is able to hold any one in the field of vision long enough to describe it.

The psychometer is clairvoyant, that is, he sees with the inner eye (of the soul.) Unless, his will-power is strong enough, and he be thoroughly trained to that particular phenomena, and his knowledge of the capabilities of his sight is profound, his perception of places, persons and events must necessarily be confused. But in case of mesmerization, in which this same clairvoyant faculty is developed, the operator, whose will holds that of the subject under control, can force him to concentrate his attention upon a given picture long enough to observe all its minute details.

There are two kinds of magnetizations. The first is purely *animal;* the other transcendant and depending on the will and knowledge of the mesmerizer, as well as on the degree of spirituality of the subject and his capacity to receive the impression of the astral light. But now it is next to ascertain that clairvoyance depends a great deal more on the former than on the latter. To the power of an adept, like Du Potet, the most *positive* subject has to submit. If his sight is ably directed by the mesmerizer, magician or spirit, the light must yield up its most sacred records to our scrutiny; for it is a book which is ever closed to those "who see and do not perceive," on the other hand, it is ever open for one who wills to see it opened. It keeps an unmutilated record of all that was, that is, or ever will be. The minutest acts of our lives are imprinted on it, and even our very thoughts rest photographed on its eternal tablets. It is the book which we see opened by the angel in the "Revelations," which is the book of life, out of which the dead are judged "according to their works." It is, in short, the *memory of God.*

Soul.

Plato, Anaxagoras, Pythagoras, and the Eleatic schools of Greece, as well as the old Chaldean sacerdotal colleges, all taught the doctrine of the dual evolution, the transmigration of souls referring only to the progress of man from world to world after death here. Every philosopher worthy of the name taught that the spirit of man, if not the soul, was pre-existent. "The Essenes," says Josephus, "believed that souls were immortal, and that they descended from ethereal space to be chained to bodies." Philo Judæus says, "the air is full of them (of souls); those which are nearest the earth descending to be tied to mortal bodies, and return to other bodies, being desirous to live in them." Nothing is eternal and unchangeable save the concealed Deity. Everything must either progress or recede; it cannot remain stationary.

A spirit which thirsts after a reunion with its soul, which alone confers upon it immortality, must purify itself through cyclic transmigrations onward toward the land of bliss and eternal rest." According to the Sohar, all souls are dual, and while the latter is a feminine principle, the spirit is masculine; that the soul could not bear this light but for the luminous mantle which she puts on; for just as the soul, when sent to this earth, puts on an earthly garment

to present herself here, so she receives above a shining garment, in order to be able to look, without injury, into the mirror, whose light proceeds from the Lord of light. While imprisoned in the body a man is a trinity, unless his pollution is such as to have caused his divorce from the soul, which may desert the spirit for the crimes and wickedness done when in the body. "Woe to the spirit which prefers to her divine husband (soul) the earthly wedlock with her terrestrial body."

"All souls which have alienated themselves in heaven from the Holy One, have thrown themselves into an abyss, at their very existence, and have anticipated the time when they are to descend on earth. * * It carries a spark of the Divine Mind to guide and direct it back to God. It becomes incarnated in the flesh, and thereby it forms for itself an individual existence, to reason and think for itself, which individuality it ever retains, its intelligence rising and progressing through countless æons, periods and cycles, from sphere to sphere, until at last it returns to the bosom of the Divine Mind, whence it came. All the animal soul must of course be disintegrated of its particles before it is able to link its pure essence forever with the Immortal Spirit.

St. Paul makes man a trine—flesh, psychical existence or spirit, and the overshadowing and at the same time interior entity or soul. He maintains that there is a physical body which is sown in the corruptible, and a spiritual body that is raised in incorruptible substance. "The first man is of the earth, earthy; the second man from heaven." Plato, speaking of the soul *(psuche)*, observes that "when she allies herself to *nous* (divine substance, a god, as *psuche* as a goddess), she does everything aright and felicitously; but the case is otherwise when she attaches herself to *annoia*." What Plato calls *nous,* Paul terms the *spirit,* and Jesus makes the *heart* what Paul calls the flesh. Pythagoras makes the soul a self-moving unit, with three elements the *vous,* the *phren,* and the *thumos;* the two latter shared with brutes, the former only being his essential self. Whether Pythagoras borrowed it from Buddha or Buddha from somebody else it matters not; the esoteric doctrine is the same.

"Socrates thought that he had a *demon,* a spiritual something, which put him on the road to wisdom. He himself knew nothing, but this put him in the way to learn all." This shows that he was what is now called a clairaudent medium, speaking from knowledge from within. So was Plato when he said "there was an *Agathon* (Supreme God), who produced in his own mind a *paradeigma* of all things." He taught that in man has "the immortal principle of the soul," a mortal body, and a separate mortal kind of soul, which was placed in a separate receptacle of the body from the other! The immortal part was in the head (*Timæus*, xix, xx), the other in the trunk.

"Plato and Pythagoras," says Plutarch, "distribute the soul into two parts, the rational (*noetic*) and the irrational (*agnoia*.) That part of the soul of man which is rational is eternal; for though it be not God, yet it is the product of an eternal Deity; but that part of the soul which is divested of reason (*agnoia*) dies."

"Man," says Plutarch, "is compound; and they are mistaken who think him to be compounded of two parts only; for they imagine that the understanding is a part of the soul; but they err in this no less than those who make the soul to be a part of the body, for the understanding (*nous*), which as far exceeds the soul as the soul is better and diviner than the body. Now this composition of soul (*vous*) with the understanding (*nous*) makes reason; and with the body passion; of which one is the beginning of the principle of pleasure and pain, and the other of virtue and vice. Of these three parts, conjoined and compacted together, the earth has given the body, the moon the soul, and the sun the understanding of the generation of man."

"The *dæmonium* of Socrates was this *vous* mind, spirit or understanding of the divine in it. This *nous* of Socrates," says Plutarch, "was pure, and mixed itself with the body no more than necessity required. * * * Every soul hath some portion of *vous* reason; a man cannot be a man without it; but as much of each soul as is mixed with flesh and appetite is changed, and through pain or pleasure becomes irrational. Every soul doth not mix herself after one sort. Some plunge themselves into the body, and so in this life their whole frame is corrupted by appetite and passion; others are mixed as to some part. But the purer part (*nous*) still re-

mains *without the body*. It is not drawn down into the body, but swims above and touches (overshadows) the extremest part of the man's head. It is like a cord to hold up and direct the subsiding part of the soul, as long as it proves obedient and is not overcome by the appetites of the flesh. The part that is plunged into the body is called *soul*. But the incorruptible part is called the *nous* and the *vulgar think it is within them*, as they likewise imagine the image reflected from a glass to be in the glass. But the more intelligent, who know it to be without, call it a *dæmon* (a god or spirit)."

"The soul, like to a dream, flies quick away, which it does not immediately as soon as it is separated from the body, but afterward when it is alone and divided from the understanding (*nous*) * * * The soul being molded and formed by the understanding (*nous*), and itself molding and forming the body by embracing it on every side, receives from it an impression and form; so that although it be separated both from the understanding and the body, it nevertheless so retains still its figure and resemblance for a long time that it may with good right be called its image."

Plato (in Laws X) defines soul as "the motion that is able to move itself. Soul is the most ancient of all things, and the commencement of motion. Soul was generated prior to body, and body is posterior and secondary, as being according to nature, ruled over by the ruling soul. The soul, which administers all things that move in every way, administers likewise the heavens.

"Soul, then, leads everything in heaven and on earth and in the sea, by its movements, the names of which are, to will, to consider, to take care of, to consult, to form opinions true and false, to be in a state of joy, sorrow, confidence, fear, hate, love, together with all such primary movements as are allied to these. * * Being a goddess herself, she ever takes as an ally *nous*, a god, and disciplines all things correctly and happily. But when with *annoia*, not *nous*, it works out everything the contrary."

Pythagoras, Plato, Timæus of Locris, and the whole Alexandrian school, derived the soul from the Universal World Soul; and the latter was, according to their own teachings, ETHER —something of such a fine nature as only to be perceived by our *inner sight*. Therefore it cannot be the essence of the *monas* or *cause*, because the *anima mundi* is but the effect, the objective emanation, of the former. But the human spirit and soul are pre-existent; but while the former exists as a distinct entity, an individualization, the soul exists as pre-existing matter, an unscient portion of an intelligent whole. Both were originally formed from the Eternal Ocean of Light; but, as the Theosophists expressed it, there is a visible as well as invisible spirit. They made a difference between the *anima bruta* and the *anima divina*.

Empedocles firmly believed all men and all animals to possess two souls; Aristotle, we find, calls one the reasoning soul *(vois)*, and the other the animal soul *(ψυχη)*. According to these philosophers, the reasoning soul came from *without* the Universal Soul, and the other from *within*. This divine and superior region, in which they located the supreme Deity, was considered by them (by Aristotle himself) as a fifth element, purely spiritual and divine; whereas the *anima mundi* proper was considered as composed of a fine igneous and ethereal nature spread throughout the universe, in short, *ether*. The Stoics, the greatest materialists of ancient days, excepted the invisible God and Divine Soul (spirit) from any such a corporeal nature. Their modern commentators and admirers, greedily seizing the opportunity, built on this ground the supposition that the Stoics believed in neither God nor soul. But Epicurus, whose doctrine, militating directly against the agency of a Supreme Being and gods in the formation and government of the world, placed him far above the Stoics in atheism and materialism, taught, nevertheless, that the soul is of a fine, tender essence, formed from the smoothest, roundest and finest atoms, which description still brings us to the sublimated ether. Arnsbius, Tertullian, Irenæus and Origen, notwithstanding their Christianity, believed, with the more modern Spinoza and Hobbes, that the soul was corporeal though of a very fine nature, yet retained the form of the person while living, and could be so identified in the spirit world.

As to the human spirit, the notions of the older philosophers and mediæval Kabalists, while differing in some particulars, agreed in the whole, so that the doctrine of the one is the doctrine of the other. The most substantial difference consisted in the location of the immortal or divine spirit of man. While the ancient Neoplatonists held that the Angocides never descended hypostatically into the living man, but only shed more or less its radiance on the inner man, the astral soul, the Kabalists of the middle ages maintained that the spirit, detaching itself from the ocean of light and spirit, entered into man's soul, where it remained through life, imprisoned in the astral capsules. This difference was the result of the belief of Christian Kabalists, more or less, in the dead letter of the allegory of the fall of man. The soul, they said, became, through the fall of Adam, contaminated with the world of matter, or satan. Before it could appear with its inclosed divine spirit in the presence of the Eternal, it had to purify itself of the impurities of darkness. They compared the spirit imprisoned within the soul to a drop of water inclosed within a capsule of gelatine and thrown into the ocean; so long as the capsule remains whole the drop of water remains isolated; break the envelope and the drop becomes a part of the ocean—its individual existence has ceased. So it is with the spirit. As long as it is inclosed in its plastic mediator, or soul, it has an individual existence. Destroy the capsule, a result which may occur from the agonies of withered conscience, crime and moral disease, the spirit returns back to its original abode: its individuality is gone.

On the other hand, the philosophers who explained the "fall into generation" in their own way, viewed spirit as something wholly distinct from the soul. They allowed its presence in the astral capsule only so far as the spiritual emanation or rays of the "shining one" were concerned. Man and soul had to conquer their immortality by ascending toward the unity with which, if successful, they were kindly linked, and into which they were absorbed, so to say. The individualization of man after death depended on the spirit, not on the soul and body. Although the word "personality," in the sense in which it is usually understood, is an absurdity if applied literally to our immortal essence; still the latter is a distinct unity, immortal and natural *per se*, and, as in the case of criminals beyond redemption, when the shining thread which links the spirit to the soul from the moment of the birth of a child, is violently snapped, and the disembodied entity is left to share the fate of the lower animals, to gradually dissolve into ether, and have its individuality annihilated, even then the spirit remains a distinct being. It becomes a planetary spirit, an angel; for *the gods of pagans or the archangels of Christians*, the direct emanations of the First Cause, notwithstanding the hazardous statement of Swedenborg, never were or will be men on our planet at least; while the modern Spiritualist, like A. J. Davis and others, contend that a soul once born, ever following the law of progress, goes on ever growing wiser and better until it ascends to the seventh heaven, when it has become perfectly divested of all impurity. This leads us back to the ancient doctrine of emanation and absorption; yet even then it may retain its individuality and a remembrance of the past.

This speculation has been in all ages the stumbling block of metaphysicians. The whole esoterism of the Buddhistical philosophy is based on this mysterious teaching, understood by a few persons and so totally misunderstood by many of the most learned scholars. Even metaphysicians are inclined to confound the effect with the cause. A person may have won his immortal life and remain the same *inner self* he was on earth through eternity; but this does not imply necessarily that he must either remain the Mr. Brown or Mr. Smith he was on earth or lose his individuality. Therefore the astral soul and terrestrial body of man may, in the dark hereafter, be absorbed into the cosmical ocean of sublimated elements and cease to feel his EGO, if this EGO did not deserve to soar higher, and the divine spirit still remain an unchanged entity, though this terrestrial experience of his emanations, may be totally obliterated at the instant of separation from the body.

The Soul is Eternal.

If the spirit, or the divine portion of the soul, is pre-existent as a distinct being, from all eternity, as Origen, Sinesius, and other Christian fathers and philosophers taught; and if it is the same, and nothing more, than the metaphysically-objective soul, how can it be otherwise than eternal? And what matters it, in such a case, whether man leads an animal or pure life, if, do what he may, he can never lose his individuality? This doctrine is as pernicious in its consequences as that of vicarious atonement. Had the latter dogma, in company with the false idea that we are all immortals, been demonstrated to the world in its true light, humanity would have been bettered by its propagation. Crime and sin would be avoided, not for fear of earthly punishment or of a ridiculous hell, but for the sake of that which lies the most deeply rooted in our inner nature—the desire of an individual and distinct life hereafter; the positive assurance that we cannot win it unless we "take the kingdom of heaven by violence," and the conviction that neither human prayers nor the blood of another man will save us from individual destruction after death, unless we firmly link ourselves during our terrestrial life with our own immortal spirit—our God.

No astral soul (that is, the spiritual body), even that of a pure, good and virtuous man, is immortal in the strictest sense. "From elements it is formed, to elements it must return." Only while the soul of the wicked vanishes, and is absorbed beyond redemption, that of every other person, even moderately pure, simply changes its ethereal particles for still more ethereal ones; and while there remains in it a speck of the divine, the individual man, or rather his personal *ego*, must die in the endless course of time. "After death," says Proclus, "the soul (the spirit) continueth to linger in the aerial body (astral form) until it is entirely purified from all angry and voluptuous passions; * * then doth it put off by a *second dying* the aerial body as it did the earthly one." Whereupon the ancients say that there is a celestial body always joined with *the soul*, and which is *immortal, luminous and star-like.*

The Chaldean magi were the masters in the secret doctrine, and it was during the Babylonian captivity that the Jews learned its metaphysics as well as the practical tenets, and the immortality of the soul. Before this time the Jews believed that it was necessary to propitiate God with burnt offerings, so that they might be blessed in this life with success, they and their offspring. The Bible nowhere teaches the immortality of the soul prior to this period. Pliny mentions three schools of Magi, one that he shows to have been founded at an unknown antiquity; the other established by Osthanes and Zoroaster. These different schools, whether Magian, Egyptian or Jewish, were derived from India, or rather from both sides of the Himalayas. Many a lost secret lies buried under wastes of sands in the Gobi desert of Eastern Turkestan, and the wise men of Khotan have preserved strange traditions and knowledge of alchemy.

We must bear in mind the teachings of the old philosophers: the spirit alone is immortal— the soul *per se* is neither eternal nor divine. When linked too closely with the physical brain of its terrestrial casket, it gradually becomes a finite mind, a simple animal and sentient life-principle (the *nephesh* of the Hebrew Bible): "And God created * * * every *nephesh* (life) that moveth" (Genesis 1:21), meaning animals, and (Genesis 11:7) it is said: "And man became a *nephesh*" (living soul), which shows that the word *nephesh* was indifferently applied to *immortal* man and mortal beast. So it is evident that the common people among the Hebrews had not the slightest idea of soul and spirit, and made no difference between life, blood, and soul, calling the latter the "breath of life," using the word soul promiscuously to express life, blood, spirit and body. The philosophers and most of the modern spiritual writers make the *soul* the divine spark, while Plato and the ancients often make it the spirit.

Baron Bunsen shows that the origin of the prayers and hymns of the Egyptian Book of the Dead is anterior to Menes and belongs probably to the pro-Menite Dynasty of Abydos, between 3,100 and 4,600 years before Christ. The learned Egyptologist makes the era of Menes, or national empire, as not later than 3,056 B. C. and demonstrates that "the system of Osirian worship and mythology was already formed before the era." "We find hymns and lessons of morality identical, or nearly so, in form and expression with those delivered by Jesus in his sermon on the mount," says Bunsen. Extracts from the Hermetic books are found on the monuments and in the tombs, such as these, "To feed the hungry, give drink to the thirsty, clothe the naked, bury the dead," * * "formed the first duty of a pious man."

Back of all religions and civilizations there appears to be another still older, until we are lost in the gray mist of time that may have existed twenty or fifty thousand years ago.

The doctrine of the immortality of the soul is as old as this period (*Tablet Brit. Mus. 562*), and perhaps far older. It dates from the time when the soul was an objective being, hence when it could hardly be denied by itself; when humanity was a spiritual race and death existed not. Toward the decline of the cycle of life, the ethereal *man spirit* then fell into the sweet slumber of temporary unconsciousness in one sphere only to find himself awakening in the still brighter light of a higher one. But while the spiritual man is ever striving to ascend higher and higher toward its source of being, passing through the cycles and spheres of individual life, physical man had to descend with the great cycle of universal creation until it found itself clothed with the terrestrial garments. Thenceforth the soul was too deeply buried in its physical clothing to reassert its existence, except in the cases of those mortal spiritual natures which, with every cycle, became more rare; but now and then it cropped out in a bright character, so pure, wise and good, that they have been deified and called gods, like Jesus Christ, Zoroaster, Buddha, Confucius, etc.

The fall of Adam and Eve in the garden of Eden, by eating of the forbidden fruit, must not be looked upon it as a personal transgression of the law of God, but simply the law of dual evolution. Adam, or the first man, began his career of existence by dwelling in the garden of Eden, dressed in the celestial garment which is a "garment of heavenly light." (*Sohar, II. 29.*) But when expelled, he is "clothed" by God, or the eternal law of evolution, or necessarianism, with coats of flesh, skin and hair. It only relates to the time when the divine spark (soul, a corruscation of the spirit) was to become incarnated in the flesh, which had evolved by physical laws of progression in a series of imprisonments, from a stone up through a long line of animal developments to the body of a man; and if he will but exercise his will and call upon his deity to help him, man can transcend the powers of the angel. "Know ye not that we shall judge angels?" asked St. Paul (1 Corinthians, 6:3). "The real man is the soul (spirit)," teaches the *Sohar.* "The mystery of the earthly man is after the mystery of the heavenly man. * * * The wise can read the mysteries in the human face." (*11:76a*.)

According to the Chaldean doctrine found in the Kabala, the Jehovah of the Jews was one of the emanations of the divine essence, and was androgynous, being male and female, like all angels, double-sexed. As Brahma, the deity, manifested in the mythical Manu, or the first man born of Sway-ambhvua, or the Self-existence, is finite, so Jehovah, embodied in Adam and Eve, is but a human-god, male and female, or the realization of humanity embodied in the first man. Like the androgynous man, male and female, passive and active, created in the image of the Elohim. But these androgynes were doomed to fall and lose their powers as soon as the two halves of the duality separated. Hence we have the fall of man by eating the forbidden fruit of the tree of knowledge; he thus lost his spiritual clothing and became clothed in flesh and skin and was material, so that he could not rise from the earth. So out of the rib of the first man, Adam, sprang Eve, the first woman, by the law of MATERIALIZATION.

This idea is beautifully expressed in the Oriental religion: "When the *Central Invisible* (the Lord Ferho) saw the efforts of the divine Scintilla, unwilling to be dragged lower down into the degradation of matter, to liberate itself, he permitted it to shoot out from itself a *monad* (an ultimate atom), over which, attached to it as by the finest thread, the divine scintilla (the soul) had to watch during its ceaseless peregrinations from one to another. Thus the monad was shot down into the first form of matter and became encased in stone; then, in course of time, through the combined efforts of *living fire* and *living water*, both of which shone by their *reflection* upon the stone, the monad crept out of its prison to sunlight as a lichen, one of the lowest forms of vegetable life. From change to change it went higher and higher; the monad, with every new transformation borrowing more of the radiance of its parent scintilla, which approached it nearer at every transmigration. For " the *First Cause* had willed it to proceed in this order," and destined it to creep on higher until its physical form became once more the Adam of *dust*, shaped in the image of Adam Kadmon.

Before undergoing its last earthly transformation, the external covering of the monad, from the moment of its conception as an embryo, passes in turn once more through the phases of the several kingdoms. In its fluidic prison it assumes a vague resemblance at various periods of its gestation to plant, reptile, bird, and animal, until it becomes a human embryo. At the birth of the future man, the monad, radiating with all the glory of its immortal parent, which watches it from the seventh sphere, becomes senseless. (*See Plato's Timæus.*) "It loses all recollection of the past and returns to consciousness but gradually, when the instinct of childhood gives way to reason and intelligence. After the separation between the life-principle (astral spirit) and the body takes place (*i. e. in death*), the liberated soul, monad, exulting rejoins the mother and father spirit, with glory proportioned to the spiritual purity of the past earth-life, the Adam who has completed the circle of necessity and is freed from the last vestige of his physical encasement. Henceforth, growing more and more radiant at each step of his upward progress, he mounts the shining path that ends at the point from which he started around the GRAND CYCLE.

For each human spirit is a scintilla of the one all-pervading light, and this is in accordance to Buddhist doctrine, which is that the individual human spirits are numberless—collectively they are one, as every drop of water drawn from out the ocean is a part of it, and yet, metaphorically speaking, may have an individual existence, and still be one with the rest of the drops going to form that ocean, though it may take millions of years to find its way back whence it came; yet during all that time it retained its individuality, whether in vapor, in sap of plants or trees, or the blood of animals, until it mingled again with the waters whence it came; that this divine spirit animates the flower, the particle of granite on the mountain side, the lion and the man, when it was individualized into an intelligent, thinking soul, that followed the law of progress, and ascended higher and higher in wisdom and intelligence, until it again returned to the great *sensorum* whence it emanated.

In *Art Magic*, page 27, there is an account of a remarkable medium, a Hindoo child twelve years of age, the daughter of a noble Hindoo of high spiritual and intellectual attainments. This little child was a great writing medium. She sits on the floor with her head resting on a tripod, embracing its support with her little arms, and in this attitude she generally falls asleep for an hour, during which time sheet after sheet is written over with characters of ancient Sanscrit. The writing is done by an invisible hand without even the ordinary appliances of pens, pencil or ink. Over four volumes of these writings have been thus produced, and that in less than a period of three years Questions in simple Hindostanee are laid upon the tripod with a lot of blank paper, and the questions are answered intelligibly. In answer to several questions concerning the origin of the soul, and the doctrine of its transmigration through the forms of animals, she wrote in Sanscrit the following, which is a translation

"That the soul is an emanation from the Deity, and in its original essence is all purity, truth and wisdom, is an axiom which the disembodied learn, when the powers of the memory are sufficiently awakened to perceive the states of existence anterior to mortal birth. In the paradise of purity and love souls spring up like blossoms in the All-Father's garden of immortal beauty. It is the tendency of that divine nature, whose chief attributes are love and wisdom, heat and light, to repeat itself eternally, and mirror forth its own perfections in scintillations from itself. These sparks of heavenly fire become souls, and as the effect must share in the nature of the cause, the fire which warms into light also illuminates into light; hence the soul emanations from the Divine are all love and heat, while the illumination of light, which streams ever from the great central Sun of Being, irradiates all souls with corresponding beams of light. Born of love, which corresponds to Divine heat and warmth, and irradiated with light, which is Divine wisdom and truth, the first and most powerful soul emanations repeated the action of their Supreme Originator, gave off emanations from their own being, some higher, some lower, the highest tending upward into spiritual essences, the lowest forming particles of matter. These denser emanations, following out the creative law, aggregated into suns, satellites and worlds, and each repeating the story of creation, suns gave birth

to systems, and every member of a system became a theater of subordinate states of spiritual or material existence.

"Thus do ideas descend into forms and forms ascend into ideas. Thus is the growth, development and progress of creation endless; and thus must spirit originate and ever create worlds of matter, for the purpose of its own unfoldment."

"Will the mighty march of creation never cease? Will the cable anchored in the heart of the great mystery, Deity, stretch out forever?"

"Forever! shout the blazing suns, leaping on in the fiery orbit of their shining life, and traveling in the glittering pathway ten thousand satellites and meteoric sparks, whirling and flashing in their jeweled crowns, all embryonic germs of new young worlds that shall be. * *

"Earths that have attained to the capacity to support organic life, necessarily attract it; earths demand it, heaven supplies it. Whence? As earths groan for the leadership of superior beings to rule over them, the spirits in their distant Edens hear the whispers of the tempting serpent, the animal principle, the urgent intellect, which, appealing to the blest souls in their distant paradises, fill them with indescribable longings for change, for broader vistas of knowledge, for mightier powers; they would be as the gods and know good and evil, and in this urgent appeal of the earths for man, and this involuntary yearning of the spirit for intellectual knowledge, the union is effected between the two, and the spirit becomes precipitated into the realms of matter, to undergo a pilgrimage through the probationary states of the earths, and only to regain its paradise again by the fulfillment of that pilgrimage.

"When spirits lived as such in paradise, emanations from a spiritual deific source, they knew no sex nor reproduced their kind. * * * When they fell, and the earth, like magnetic tractors, drew them within the vortex of its grosser elements, they became what the earth compelled them to be. In the earlier ages of these growing worlds the conditions of life were rude and violent; hence the creatures on them partook of their nature. Then too first obtained the nature of sex and the law of generation. To people these earths man, like other living creatures, must reproduce his kind. All things in matter are male and female; minerals, plants, animals and men. Spirit, the creative energy, is the masculine principle that creates; nature, the passive recipient, is that which germinates; hence creation. Man must obey the law; hence sex and generation. * * *

" Man lives on many earths before he reaches this. Myriads of worlds swarm in space, where the soul in rudimental states performs its pilgrimages ere he reaches the large and shining planet named Earth, the glorious function of which is to confer *self-consciousness*. At this point only is he man; at every other stage of his vast, wild journey he is but an embryonic being; a fleeting, temporary shape of matter; a creature in which a *part*, but only a *part*, of the high imprisoned soul shines forth; a rudimental shape, with rudimental functions; ever living, dying—sustaining a littering spiritual existence as rudimental as the material shape whence it emerged; a butterfly springing up from the chrysalitic shell, but ever, as it onward rushes, in new births, new deaths, new incarnations, anon to die and live again, but still stretch upward, still strive onward, still rush on the giddy, dreadful, toilsome, rugged path, until it awakens once more, once more to live and be a material shape, a thing of dust, a creature of flesh and blood, but now a *man*.

" It is from the dim memory that the soul retains first of its original brightness and fall, next of its countless migrations through the various undertones of beings that antedate its appearance on this earth as man, that the belief in the doctrine of the metempsychosis (transmigration of the souls through the animal kingdoms) has arisen. Yet it is a sin against divine truth to believe that the exalted soul that has once reached the dignity and upright stature of manhood should or could retrograde into the bodies of creeping things or crouching animals —not so, not so!

" In the fleeting images which antecedent states leave on the spiritual brain, in the half effaced and half-imperfect perceptions of existence which each new stage of progress and each successive journey through various lower earths leave, like an unquiet, ill-remembered dream, on the spirit's consciousness, the past becomes confused with the present, and something of what we have been imposes its shadow across the path of the future, as a dim possibility of what we may be.

" After the soul's birth into humanity it acquires self-consciousness, knowledge of its own individuality, and closing up forever its career of material transformations with the death of the mortal body, it gravitates on to a fresh series of existences in purely spiritual realms of being. Here the further purifications of the soul commence anew, commences with that sublime attribute of self-knowledge which enables even the wickedest spirit to enjoy and profit by the change; for memory supplies him with lessons which urge him to struggle forward into conquest over sin, and prophetic sight stimulates him to aspire until he shall attain, by well directed effort, the sublime hights of purity and goodness from which he fell to become a mortal pilgrim.

" The triumphant souls who enter heaven by effort are God's *ministering angels* of power, wisdom, strength and beauty. The dwellers in primal states of Eden are only spirits. The first are God-men, heavenly men—strong and mighty powers — thrones, dominions, worldbuilders, glorious hierarchies of sun, bright souls, who never more can fall. Spirits are but the breath, the spark, the shadow of a god; angels are gods in person. * *

" During the various transitional states of the soul in passing through the myriads of forms and myriads of earths, whereon their probations are outwrought, the changes are all effected by a process analogous to human death. During the period that subsists ere the soul, expelled from one material shape, enters another, the drifting spirit, still enveloped by the magnetic aural body which binds it to the realm of matter, becomes for its short term of intermediate spiritual existence an ELEMENTARY SPIRIT."

CHAPTER IV.

MEDIUMS, ANCIENT AND MODERN

Prophets, Seers, Magicians, Soothsayers, Astrologers, Fortune-Tellers, Materializations, Raps, Trances.

From the earliest history of man down to the present time some persons have been possessed of great psychological powers, and have in all countries held the position of prophets, seers, magicians, soothsayers, astrologers, medicine-men and fortune-tellers. Many of them have been exposed in their tricks, while others have stood out in bold relief as possessing a power of divining the future and telling the past, revealing facts and incidents that no one could have known, or were only in possession of the dead

There appears to be a great variety of gifts and powers possessed by these persons. Some are developed in one specialty, and others in something different; but they all point in one direction, and claim that man exists after death, that the spirit or life-principle of man lives beyond the grave, whether it be from the teachings of the Bible, Rig-Veda, Heremetic books of ancient Egypt, the Zend-Avesta of Persia, the Koran or the Book of Mormon. Their priests and priestesses are millions, and their churches, temples and pagodas lift their spires in every land; and the great majority of all people in all nations have a religion and a belief in the immortality of the soul. Man is a religious animal, and it arises from a feeling within that he cannot smother or keep down. It ever rises up and reaches out and will contemplate and think of the future, a life in the spirit world. He sees the dead bodies of his friends and relations laid in the cold grave; but he cannot reconcile his mind, his reason, to the belief that that is the last of him. The body will return to the dust from which it came, but whither has gone the life, the intelligence that once animated the cold remains? He sees the birds flying through the air, and the smoke rise from the burning logs that were once living trees;

they are shortly consumed by the fire, there is only a small pile of ashes left; what has become of the rest? The smoke has disappeared in the skies; so, he says, must the life, the intelligence of his friends have gone the same way. There must be some place where all these things have gone; there must be a great reservoir for all; there must be an invisible world as well as a visible world. Where it is, or how it is, we cannot tell; but it must exist; it cannot be lost; there is no annihilation of anything; it has only changed its condition; that is all.

The evidence given by the mediums is overwhelming, if we can rely on their statements as true, as they have in all ages been put to the severest test, but it is something seen, heard and felt, that is not capable of explanation or demonstration upon any scientific basis known to man; and those who have not that peculiar power, which compose the largest number, are not willing that a thing can be seen, heard and felt by some and not by all.

And here lies the great difficulty to make them believe, for they are not willing to admit that others have higher perception and can see, hear and see things that they cannot; therefore they remain incredulous and skeptical. And there are some whose moral and religious organs are so low that the question might be, have they evolved to the condition of spiritual beings, or are they still man-like apes?

There is something very remarkable about this psychic force, or spiritual manifestations, that will not act in the presence of some persons while it will make itself apparent with others. With some it derives force and power, while with others it weakens and will not act. There is something in their nature or aura that repels the spirit, like that of the negative pole of the magnet; and especially where the mind is firmly set, in opposition, of a positive nature—not that of disbelief, but a fixed purpose not to believe.

Persons who possess this mediumship power are very sensitive, and have a large amount of electricity in their bodies, which generate this force like the electric eel; and some have it so strong that they are able to give a slight shock which thrills down the spine, and are able to light a jet of gas with the end of their fingers.

The mind of the investigator should be kept untrammeled, free from the influence of men, authority, prejudice or passion, so that it may have free scope in the investigation of facts and laws which exist and are established in nature, and is the grand antecedent necessity to scientific discovery and permanent progress. And until men of science can come forth and investigate the phenomena of spiritualism in that light, like Hare, De Morgan, Brookes, Wallace, De Gasparin, Thury, Wagner and Butlerof, etc. they will never succeed. These men had the manhood to admit the phenomena, and have struggled to solve the mystery and see if it has any relation to the existence of men's hereafter; and the only solution they can find is, that the word comes back that "man lives and exists beyond the grave," and that intelligence never dies, that like matter and force it is indestructible.

In this age of cold reason and prejudice even the church has to look to science for help to support her tottering creeds; when in reality these manifestations are the same as those in the Bible, and go to explain it and establish the fact beyond a doubt of the immortality of the soul. But the church is so blindly roped up in her creeds and dogmas that she is not willing to admit these facts, which come as further evidence and as a new addition to the good old book, but contend that it is sealed and that the days of miracles and manifestation of the spirit are gone by, and that there are to be no more revelations; that those given in the dim mists of the past are sufficient, and that it is blasphemy to pretend to say that there can be anything more given from on high.

Yet science and reason will tell us that if those marvelous powers ever existed, they can be repeated now; that the laws of God, which are the laws of nature, are unchangeable, and have always existed and will forever exist. But these new revelations tend to interfere with some of the established rules and tenets of the church and the teachings of modern Christianity, which have widely departed from those taught by the founders, for her representatives have poisoned the waters of simple faith, and now humanity mirrors itself in waters made turbid with all the mud stirred up from the bottom of the once pure shrine. The anthropomorphic God of our fathers is replaced by anthropomorphic monsters, whose ripples send back the distorted images of truth and facts, as evoked by its misguided imagination.

Those who are *soul-blind* are constitutionally incapable of distinguishing psychological causes from material effects, as the color-blind are to select scarlet from purple. There is often wanting a development of that brain matter in certain things, as to make the person perfectly incompetent to understand that subject; as with some persons who have no taste or liking for mathematics, and no teaching or explanation can ever make them mathematicians, and it is a waste of time to try and teach them, though they may have ability in other branches of science. So it is with many men; they have no development in those organs of the brain that tend to elevate them above the cold atheist. They are perfectly destitute of the higher faculties that lift man above the brute creation, as these organs stand higher and are nearer related to wisdom than reason.

Reason being a faculty of our physical brain, one which is justly defined as that of deducing inferences from premises, and being wholly dependent on the evidence of other senses, cannot be a quality pertaining directly to our divine spirit. Hence all reasoning which implies discussion and argument would be useless, as reason has been substituted by man for that of intuition or instinct in the lower order of animals, and has so got control of mind as to discard anything that cannot be solved by its test. Therefore it is difficult to reason on religion, but it must be looked upon with blind faith, as it will not stand any of the tests known to science, so we are forced to accept it as it is revealed to us by those gifted with those divine powers which belong to prophets, seers and mediums, whose minds possess that quickness of perception, sight, hearing and feeling that belong to the soul.

Logic shows us that as mind as well as matter had a common origin it must have attributes in common, and as the vital and divine spark in man's material body is the causation, so it must lurk in every subordinate species. The latent mentality which in the lower kingdoms is recognized as a semi-consciousness, consciousness and instinct, is largely subdued in man. Reason, the out-growth of the physical brain, developes at the expense of instinct—the flickering reminiscence of a once divine omniscience —spirit. Reason, the badge of the sovereignty of physical man over all other physical organisms, is often put to shame by the instinct of an animal. As his brain is more perfect than that of any other creature, its emanations most naturally produce the highest results of mental action. But reason avails only for the consideration of mental things. It is capable of helping its possessor to a knowledge of spirit.

In losing instinct man loses his intuitional powers, which are the crown and ultimatum of instinct. Reason is the clumsy weapon of science—intuition the unerring guide of the seer. Instinct teaches plant and animal their season for the procreation of their species, and guides the dumb brute to find its appropriate remedy in the hour of sickness. Reason, the pride of man, fails to check the propensities of his nature, and brooks no restraint upon the unlimited gratification of his senses. Far from leading him to be his own physician, its subtile philosophies lead him too often to his own destruction. Woman possesses less reason than man, and relies more on her intuition. Her perception is therefore quicker than man's, and she lives a purer and better life morally and physically; therefore she makes the best MEDIUM, for she relies upon intuition rather than reason.

Every human being is born with the rudiment of the inner sense called *intuition*, which may be developed into what the Scotch know as "second sight." All the great philosophers, Plotinus, Porphyry and Iamblicus, employed this faculty, and taught the doctrine. "There is a faculty of the human mind," writes Iamblichus, " which is superior to all which is born or begotten. Through it we are enabled to attain union with the superior intelligences, to being transported beyond the scenes of this world, and to partaking the higher life and peculiar powers of the heavenly ones." All great mentalities possess that power. It is that which lifted Homer and Shakespeare above the common herd of humanity.

To this *inner sight* or intuition the Jews owe their Bible and the Christians their New Testament. For what Moses and Jesus said and wrote and gave to the world was the fruit of their intuition or illumination, that bears the marks of modern Spiritualism, for Christ was a medium of the highest order. He could see, hear and talk with spirits. All the spirit world appeared at his command—the physical, intellectual and spiritual. He could multiply the loaves and fishes, see into the hearts of men as well as into the water to tell the fishermen where to cast their nets. He could still the tempest; cure the sick, lame and blind; and cast out devils—evil spirits that had got possession of men.

Were it not for this intuition, undying though often wavering because it is so clogged with matter, man's life would be a parody and humanity a fraud. This ineradicable feeling of the presence of something *outside* and *inside* ourselves is one that no dogmatic contradictions nor external form of worship can destroy in humanity, let scientists and clergymen do what they may. Moved by such thoughts of the boundlessness and impersonality of the Deity, Gautama-Buddha exclaimed: "As the four rivers which fall into the Ganges lose their names as soon as they mingle their waters with the holy river, so all who believe in Buddha cease to be Brahmans." It is the same thing that forced the Psalmist to cry out, "I know that my Redeemer lives." It has led men to the stake and supported them in the most trying hours.

"The gods exist," says Epicurus, "but they are not what the rabble suppose them to be." "But neither the FIRST GREAT CAUSE, nor its emanation—human-immortal spirit—have left themselves without a witness." Mesmerism, modern Spiritualism and occultism are there to attest the great truths of the immortality of the soul. * * * The Pythagorean knowledge of things and the profound erudition of the Gnostics, the world and time-honored teachings of the great philosophers of antiquity, were all rejected as doctrines of Antichrist.

The last seven wise men of the Orient, the remnant group of the Neoplatonic philosophy, were Hermios, Piscious, Diogenes, Eulalius, Damoskius, Simplicius and Isidorus, who fled from the fanatical persecutions of Justinian to Persia. The reign of wisdom then closed on Europe for over fifteen centuries. The books of Thoth (or Hermes Trismagistus), which contain within their sacred pages the spiritual and physical history of the creation and progress of our world, were left to mold in oblivion and contempt for ages. But by the untiring research of Champollion, Max Muller and others, the Oriental learning has been resurrected from a night of oblivion. Though shrouded in mystery and cabalistic signs, that were intended ever to keep the secret from the knowledge of the ignorant rabble.

"Magic, which is based on the existence of a mixed world of forces placed within not without us, and with which we can enter into communication by the use of certain arts and practices; * * an element existing in nature unknown to most men; which gets hold of persons and withers and breaks them down as the fearful hurricane does a bulrush. It scatters men far away; it strikes them in a thousand places at the same time, without their perceiving the invisible foe or being able to protect themselves. * * All this is demonstrated; but that this element could choose friends and select favorites, obey their thoughts, answer to the human voice, and understand the meaning of traced signs—that is what people cannot realize and what their reason rejects; and that is what I saw. And I say it here most emphatically, that to me it is a fact and a truth demonstrated forever." (Du Potet, *Magie Devoilee*, pp. 57, 149.)

This power was well known to the ancients. What is now called nervous fluid or magnetism the men of old called *occult power*, or the potency of the soul subjection to magic; which power Christ possessed, as he cast out devils by it. And it is evident that he must have got initiated into the mysteries while in Egypt, or from some of the magicians of Chaldea, who were great adepts in the art, which is now beginning to be known and revered; and it throws great light on the miracles of the Bible and explains away the strange stories of witches, ghosts, spooks and apparitions, and the miracles that Jesus Christ and his apostles performed. It is evident from the writings of the New Testament that these magicians had something to do with the birth of Christ, for they were the wise men from the East that followed the star to Bethlehem.

Professor Dominico Berti, in his life of Bruno, says: "In common with the Alexandrian Platonists and the later Kabalists, held that Jesus Christ was a great magician in the sense given to this appellation by Porphyry and Cicero, who called it the *divina sapientea* (divine knowledge); and Philo Judæus, who described the Magi as the most wonderful inquirers into the hidden mysteries of nature, not in the degrading senses given now-a-days. The Magi spoken of in the Bible were holy men, who, setting themselves apart from everything else on earth, contemplated the divine virtues and understood the divine nature of the gods and spirits the more clearly. So they initiated others into the same mysteries, which consist in one holding an interrupted intercourse with those invisible beings during life. Magic in this sense is a higher order of religion, in which the adept is enabled to hold converse with spirits and angels, which are a higher order of spirits who have progressed in the spirit world."

Mediumship.

There are two classes of mediums. One class—the high, the holy, the pure, the good—may be called properly *mediators*, for they come between the godlike principle and man. The other class is composed of those who use this power for gain, who descend to the low purpose of using this gift to accomplish bad and wicked deeds—revenge, malice, debauchery, lust, vice and crime. In either case it is a gift of nature, at birth or subsequently, modified so that the person's aura will attract those influences that so strangely manifest themselves in the different mediums.

To BE A MEDIATOR or good medium, it is necessary for the persons to be pure and good men and women, or they will draw to themselves bad influences, as "like attracts like;" and the good spirits gather around the good mediums who live pure lives, while the bad mediums gather bad spirits. So that it all depends on the medium as to what kind of communications one gets God-men, like Christ, Apollonius, Iamblichus, Plotinus and Porphyry, gathered this heavenly nimbus around them that sent forth wisdom and goodness like rays of light, to teach men to be better, to overcome the temptations of the flesh, and to aspire to a purer and better life around them, evolved by the power of their own pure souls. The best and most exalted spirits were ever ready to assist them in all that was good and noble.

It is asserted that Apollonius, on account of his abstemious life, could see "the present and the future in a clear mirror," while Christ could read the hearts of men and hold converse with angels; which would be the condition of all men if they possessed that high and exalted nature A few in all ages of the world have had that gift; but they have all been men and women of great purity of soul and the most abstemious in habits. And the great seventy, like the fakirs of India, by their self-denial and torture of the body, and the mortification of the flesh, were enabled to perform wonders

Plotinus taught that there is in the soul a living principle which attracts it onward and upward to its origin and center, *the Eternal God,* and this accounts for the cause why all admire the pure and good man, for in the lowest and most depraved there is a divine spark that is pure, yet it is so loaded down with vile and bad matter that it is difficult for it to do right; and for that reason he can comprehend the sublime truth of right and justice which he so much admires in others, but has not the moral courage to emulate, and is forced by his base passions, not willing to submit to the self-denial and discipline that others possess, which elevates them.

But when a medium defiles the temple in which dwells the spirit of the living God, the temple becomes polluted by the admission of evil passions, thoughts and desires, the medium falls into the sphere of sorcery. The door is opened, the pure spirits retire and the evil ones rush in. They will no more mingle in the spirit world than they will here The sorcerer, like the pure magician, forms his own aura and subjects to his will congenial yet inferior spirits,

who assist him in his performances and in carrying out his evil designs on man.

There is a class of weak-minded men, women and children who give themselves up to be controlled by bad spirits, who so get control of the person as to make them do as they please. Ignoring their own individuality they blindly follow the promptings of these evil spirits, and often allow them to guide and so control them that they commit crimes and do many wicked things, so they have been called possessed with devils, or more properly speaking, evil spirits, and in certain cases they have been obsessed, as in the case of Mary Magdalen.

This class of mediums is always passive, whether beneficent or maleficent; and happy are the pure in heart, who repel unconsciously by that very clearness of their inner nature the dark, evil spirits; for verily they have no other weapon of defense but that inborn goodness and purity.

Mediumship, as it is often practiced now-a-days, is a more undesirable gift than the robe of Nessus; and it is what has brought Spiritualism into disrepute, and caused it to be shunned by many; for when it descends to that of sorcery, witchcraft, the black arts and voodooism, it is to be deprecated, and should be punished with the severity of the law For it brings around bad influences that are likely to mislead weak-minded persons.

True and pure mediums must be properly tested by the communications given, and all communications must be closely scrutinized by the light of reason and justice As St John says (1 Epistle, chap. iv): "Believe not every spirit; but try the spirits, whether they are of God, many false prophets have gone out into the world " The ancient witches and familiar spirits generally turned their gift to a trade; like the Obeah woman of En-dor, though she may have killed her fatted calf for Saul, accepted hire from other visitors.

In India, the jugglers, who by the way are less avaricious than many modern mediums, and the Essana, or sorcerer and serpent-charmers, of Asia and Africa, all exercise their gifts for money. Not so with the mediators and hierophants. "Buddha was a mendicant and refused his father's throne." "The Son of man had not where to lay his head " The chosen apostles provided "neither gold nor silver nor brass in their purses." Apollonius gave one-half of his fortune to his relatives, the other half to the poor. Iamblichus and Plotinus were renowned for charity and self-denial; the fakirs, or holy mendicants of India, never take pay; the Pythagoreans, Essenes and Theraputæ, believed their hands would be defiled by the touch of money. When the apostles were offered money to impart their spiritual powers, refused. Peter, though a coward and three times denied his Savior, still indignantly spurned the offer, saying, "Thy money perish with thee, because thou hast thought that the gift of God may be purchased with money." These men were good mediums or mediators, guided merely by their own personal spirit or divine soul, and availing themselves of the help of good spirits, so far as they directed them in the right path, ever guided by the prompting arising from a pure heart.

Apollonius spurned the sorcerers and "common soothsayers," and declared that it was his peculiar abstemious mode of life which gave gave him such powers. Professor Wilder believed with Iamblichus in the attaining of divine power, "which, overcoming the mundane life, rendered the individual an organ of the Deity." Plotinus, when asked to attend the public worship of the gods, said, "It is for them (the spirits) to come to me." That the will of the pure man will command the spirits as well as other matter, and that our souls can attain communion with the highest intelligences, with "natures loftier than itself," and carefully drive away from his theurgical ceremonies every inferior spirit or bad demon, which he taught his disciples to recognize. Jesus declared man the lord of the sabbath, and at his command the terrestrial and elementary spirits fled from their temporary abodes—a power which was shared by Apollonius and many of the Brotherhood of the Essenee of India and Mount Carmel.

The ancient Jews in the time of Moses, David and Samuel, encouraged prophecy, divination, astrology and soothsaying, and maintained schools and colleges in which the natural gifts were strengthened and developed; while witches and those who divined by the spirit of *Ob* were put to death. Even in Christ's time the poor physical mediums who were obsessed by evil spirits were driven to the tombs. It is evident that the ancierts knew the difference between the good and bad spirits, and that the latter brought ruin upon the individual and disaster upon the community.

Physical manifestations depend on the medium being passive, and spirits never control persons of a positive character, who are determined to resist all extraneous influences. When they seize upon the weak and feeble-minded they often drive their victims to vice. Physical mediums are generally sickly, or inclined to some abnormal vice; and their influence generally is of a low order of spirits or elements that are injurious to the medium; while the higher order of mediums generally enjoy good health.

A medium is only the vehicle through which the spirits display their power. The aura that served them varies day by day, and as it would appear from Prof. Crookes' experiments, even hour by hour. It is an external effect resulting from interior causes. The medium's moral state determines the kind of spirits that come; and the spirits come reciprocally, influence the medium intellectually, physically and morally. The perfection of the mediumship is in ratio to his passivity, and the danger he incurs is in equal degree. When he is fully "developed," perfectly passive, his own astral spirit may be benumbed and even crowded out of his body, which is then occupied by an elemental, or, what is worse, by a human fiend of the eighth sphere, who proceeds to use it as his own organism, and often drives the medium unconsciously to commit some diabolical crime, to even sacrifice her own child.

The adepts in occultism claim the power to bring to their aid the occult forces in nature, which assists them, and without that power they could do nothing; that they command these forces to help them, and it is by learning how to control them that they are enabled to perform such things; that the invisible intelligences are at their command, and the secret is to know how to command them; but that these life-forces or principles can only be used by certain manipulators. It is different from Spiritualism, hence they control the forces, while in the latter the forces control the medium. It may be possible, in the case of occultism, that the adept may be deceived and be controlled by a higher spirit. And that there are two classes of forces, one which is under the control of the good, virtuous and wise, which requires great severity, the observance of rigid rules of sobriety, abstinence, cleanliness, purity of soul and body, the observance of fixed times for meditation or prayer, abstraction, when the soul can go out into the ether and associate with those who have long since passed away; that a mind thus influenced can travel on the wings of electricity, which is its vehicle, to the remotest parts of the earth in a few seconds. The astral soul is a separate and distinct entity of our *ego*, and can roam far away from the body without breaking the thread of life, that time and space do not enter into its wanderings, that it can traverse the earth like an electric spark.

The adept knows the nature of the soul—a form composed of nervous fluid and atmospheric ether—and knows how the vital force can be made active or passive at will, so long as there is no final destruction of some necessary organ. Graffarilus claims that every object in nature that is not artificial, when once burned to ashes, still retains that form in the ashes. Kircher, Digby and Vallemont hold that forms of plants could be resuscitated from their ashes. At a meeting of naturalists in 1834, at Stuttgart, a receipt for producing such experiments was found in a work of Oetinger. Ashes of burned plants contained in vials, when heated, exhibited again their various forms. "A small obscure cloud gradually rose in the vial, took a definite form and presented to the eye the flower or plant." "The earthly husk," wrote Oetinger, "remains in the retort, while the volatile essence ascends, *like a spirit*, perfect in form but void of substance."

And if the astral form of a plant, when its body is dead, still lingers in its ashes, as has been shown by chemists, by the application of heat, will skeptics persist in saying that the soul of *man*, the *inner ego*, after the death of the grosser form, is at once dissolved and is no more? "At death," says a philosopher, "the one body exudes from the other by osmose through the brain; it is held near its old garment by a double attraction, physical and spiritual, until the latter decomposes. And if the proper conditions are given, the soul can reinhabit it

and resume the suspended life. It does it in sleep; it does it more thoroughly in trance. Most surprisingly at the command and with the assistance of the Heremetic adept, Iamblichus declared that a person endowed with such resuscitating power is 'full of God.' All the subordinate spirits of the upper spheres are at his command, for he is no longer a mortal, but himself a god. In his Epistle to the Corinthians, Paul remarks that "the *spirits* of the prophets are subject to the prophets."

"If the molecules of the cadaver are imbued with the physical and chemical forces of the living organism, what is to prevent them from being again set in motion, provided we know the nature of the vital force and how to command it? The materialist can certainly offer no objection, for with him it is no question of reinfusing a soul. For him the soul has no existence, and the human body may be regarded simply as a vital engine, a locomotive which will start upon the application of heat and force and stop when they are withdrawn. To the theologian the case offers greater difficulties, for, in his view, death cuts asunder the tie that binds soul and body, and the one can no more be returned into the other without a miracle than the born infant can be compelled to resume its fœtal life."

But the Heremetic philosophers stand between these two irreconcilable antagonists, and are *masters of the situation*. Spirit controls the body. The life that animates the body, whether voluntarily or involuntarily, as you term it, is in reality the result of the existing spirit. Every molecule, every susceptible atom, each substance attracted in our bodies, is under the direct control of our spiritual natures. Do not mistake this for *will*; for this is not under the control of our volition. Do not mistake it for intellect. The intellect is subtile in its operations; but the spiritual nature is still more subtile, and that it is which voluntarily or involuntarily controls every atom of our physical existence. It attracts to us each substance that is necessary to make up our bodies, rejecting such as are not consistent with the form thereof, and determines the nature of our physical bodies in a great degree.

Every embodied mind possesses in embryo every germ and power that is possessed by the disembodied mind, and the disembodied mind possesses every power that is possessed by the embodied mind, with this difference, they have a physical organixation of their own, like ourselves, and, are obliged to act upon ; physical organisms here, in order to work out the manifestations of their presence and intelligence. They have the advantage of possessing greater elasticity of will, of acting upon more minute particles of matter. than you can govern, because your actions, in connection with matter, must be directed exclusively by the motions of your physical body. The spirit, on the other hand, has a more subtle will, and, being constrained by no physical body, can act upon more nearly ultimated particles of matter, and thereby produce effects which defy physical science, and which scientific men fail to understand, for they do not understand the laws by which they exist; they cannot explain by what power the muscles are contracted, by which the hand is moved, and as to how a table can be moved by an invisible force, is impossible— yet it is the same hidden force, the same will-power of the spirit that accomplishes both; still, there has been a thought conveyed over the nerves that sets the muscles to work, and the brain is moved by the spirit that has set it to work to send out the thought that travels over the nerves that causes the muscles to move.

The spirits see the aura around physical bodies that you do not. They see the action of the nervous fluids, and know from its sight that these nervous fluids are composed of infinitesimal globules, each one corresponding to its particular function, which the spirit employs when it raps on the table, or produces vibrations of the atmosphere. The infinitesimal molecules that are thus employed might be called vacuums; and in these minute globules of atmosphere or aura resides the power, not only of communications, but to lift tables ard project bodies through the atmosphere. And it is owing to this atmosphere or aura that surrounds the person or thing that enables the spirit to communicate to mortal beings.

Materialization.

The materialization of a spirit is only gathering around it the atoms that are in the aura and atmosphere around the medium, from whom it draws the material to render its form visible, to embodied souls or living human beings. The spirit having the form and the intelligence is soon able, under proper conditions, to make itself visible. As the red and yellow rays are strong and antagonistic they have a tendency to scatter the atoms of matter, so materialization has to be done in the dark or in blue rays of light where all other rays but the blue are excluded. So when spirits wish to materialize they draw from the air, which is the great reservoir of inorganic matter, such material as light will not show in a clear sun light but in the dark it gives off a pale light. When all the rays of light are reflected the object is white, when all are absorbed the object is black.

Myrids of animals exist that can not be seen with the naked eye because they are too small or have not the coloring matter to reflect the rays of light.

The body generates an aura through the pores of the skin by a process of endosmose action, is then thrown off by an exosmose action in the form of carbonic acid gas, which is poisonous if again returned to the human system, but under the manifestations of the spirit there is, accompanying this carbonic acid gas, a certain force or power. whieh, for the lack of a better term, we call *nerve-aura*. It is a similar force that vibrates along the nervous system of the human body, and it is upon this substance that the spirit acts to produce a sound. Nitrogen is the most subtle of all elemental properties of the atmosphere. Carbonic acid gas, mingled with nitrogen in atomic proportions, becomes the material whereby spirit-lights and vibrations are produced, by the aid of electricity. These vibrations occur in direct connection with certain conditions known to the world but which is unknown to science, because it has no instruments fine enough to make an analysis of these powers; and the best physical manifestations are when the medium is confined in a room where the air is foul with carbonic acid gas, though it may be injurious to the health of those living in the body; but out of this foul air the spirits can find the best materializing matter to build up visible forms; and it has been discovered by photographing that blue and violet light is the best for taking pictures, as it is the most harmonious and slowest, as it fills all space and gives color to the sky and a fine effect on the picture, and has none of the antagonistic properties of the red and yellow rays which impede the action of the spirits, so all seances should be held in rooms lit up by blue or violet rays of light. The artist requires the same kind of rays so that it will fix the picture on the plate, from which he is able, by chemicals, to transfer to another. And all the spirit requires is the proper conditions and similar lights to form a body that is visible to the natural eye. The picture is there and the spirit is there; but it requires the proper materials to bring them out, so that they become visible to the mortal eye. And in this way spiritual pictures are taken, as well as those of living persons. And if pictures can be taken by one kind of light and not another, why not materialization be effected likewise?

All light has a dematerializing effect. Spirits find it much easier to form in the dark, as all plating and impressions of the photographer have first to be set in the dark. The picture is given by the light shaded with blue screens and skylight; and, as the photographer has to use his dark cabinet to set the image in the glass, so has the medium to use the dark cabinet to enable the spirit chemist to build up and plate anew the spirit with visible matter before it can appear in the light.

The spirit, having once lived in the flesh, has learned the laws of the flesh, and knows how to control even the organisms of other and living bodies. The spirit is the life principle of the body. It is what steam is to the engine— which is dead matter, but, as soon as the steam is turned on the piston moves backward and forward, giving life to the whole. so, when the spirit leaves the body, it is cold, dead matter; but when the spirit enters, it at once gives life and animation. The spirit and the body are nucleus around which all matter clings, so that when a spirit wishes to materialize it has but little to do but draw the required matter from others and the air, and in that way it makes itself a visible body.

The human body is always giving off atoms of matter through the pores of the skin so that every seven years, and some say, every nine months, the whole of the body has passed away and has been replaced by new matter. "We live," says Herbert Spencer, "by constantly dieing." These atoms given from the body, especially from the medium's, is used by the spirits, who understand their chemical nature, and recompose them around, the spirit which is a perfect form to build upon. Like copper and zinc, under a strong current power or a circle of spirits, which induces them to yield those atoms, which the spirit chemist employs to materialize forms by the use of elements in the air which are as simple and well understood by the spirits as electrotyping is by mortals, so that the spirit can accomplish in a few minutes what in the flesh requires years to build up, the difference being one of time and of permanency. It is a process of galvanizing over the spiritual body with visible matter, that enables them to show themselves to us in the flesh. As the spiritual body is invisible to the natural sight, but can be seen only by the clairvoyant, who sees with the vision of the soul, to enable the spirit to be seen by the mortal eye it must clothe itself in material matter that reflects light.

The hand being full of nerves more readily materializes than any other part of the body, and this accounts for the many hands often seen at a seance, and is generally the first part of the body that materializes.

Materialization is the highest realization of modern Spiritualism. It brings the living face to face with those who were supposed to be dead. They tell us that they still live, and have only shed off the outward husk, the mortal body. It is the strongest evidence of the immortality of the soul. The body is only one of the stages of development of the embryotic conditions of the soul, which had passed through the lower forms of life during gestation, that, like the eagle and the butterfly, has broken through the shell of mortality and mounts on wings into the sky, no longer feeding on the gross things of the earth, but draws its life and vitality from the ether.

The same knowledge and control of occult forces, including the vital forces which enable a fakir temporarily to leave and then re-enter his body. Jesus, Apollonius and Elijah were able to recall their several subjects to life, made it possible for the ancient hierophants to animate statues and cause them to act and speak.

It is the same knowledge and power which made it possible for Paracelsus to create his homunculi; for Aaron to change his rod into a serpent and a budding branch; for Moses to cover Egypt with frogs and other pests, and the same Egyptian theurgist of our day to vivify his pigmy mandragora, which has physical life but no soul. It is no more wonderful that upon presenting the necessary conditions Moses should call into life large reptiles and insects than that, under like favoring conditions, the physical scientists should call out the small ones which he names bacteria.

Nearly all the forms of phenomena of the ancients wonder-workers, recorded in sacred and profane histories, are produced now by spiritual mediums. I have seen bodies moved, hang suspended in the mid air; instruments play by laying in the hands of the medium; have felt the weight of invisible hands; heard voices in the air over my head; musical instruments flying around in the room; flowers fresh with the dew on them, handed out of a cabinet in a well lit room; have had deceased friends and relatives described to me, so perfect, and their names given so that there could be no mistake; I have been tilted out of a chair by the touch of the hand of a little cousin; I have seen a dozen ghosts or spirits walk out of a room that I had sealed up; I have seen them in the broad daylight rise up, come to me, and have felt their pulse—sometimes they had pulse and at other times they had none; I have conversed with them, they told me who they were and where they had departed this life, but they would not admit that they were dead, but said they had passed to a higher life.

I have had communications from my dear departed friends, written on a slate, held in my own hand under the table, the medium only touching it. The signature of my mother was so perfect, that, had I not known she was dead, I would have been willing to swear to its genuineness in a court of justice.

I once called upon Dr. Slade, the celebrated medium, to see if I could get some new light, and on reading an article to him on "Evolution," it met the approbation of a spirit present 'expressed by rapping on the table; but, when I read where Darwin says, "Young birds do not make as good nests as old ones," it rapped "no," and so it differed with him on that subject. Every now and then it would pat me on the thighs, which were under the table, approving the article. It was in broad daylight, and I am certain it was not done by any visible person, as the medium was the only person in the room. He then placed one hand in mine on the table, and took a slate, wiped it clean, placed a piece of pencil on it, and took another slate and laid it over it, then held the two slates up to the side of my ear. I could hear the pencil scratching like it was writing; soon it gave three taps, and then he opened the slate, and one whole side was written over in a plain, legible manner. The following is a correct copy:

DEAR SIR: Your subject is one that is little understood. Man has an intellectual nature, and also intuition, so have animals; but, unless these two are wedded, he is not a successful man. Often intellect has taken on the aid of intuition; and, again, intuition has controlled man with the guardiance of intellect. Some men fail when animals do not, he by throwing his intuition aside and glories in his intellect, and he often makes great mistakes in life. Animals have no pride in intellect, and trust more to intuition and do not fail.

A. W. SLADE.

The signature was that of his deceased wife.

The wonderful test given by Mr. Slade convinced the honest German scientist, Zollner, that there were forces unknown to the scientist, which he called *transcendental* physics.

Mr. Zollner, professor of physical astronomy at the University of Leipsic, one of the most renowned schools of learning in Europe, made many tests in a scientific way in broad daylight, in the presence of other professors, with the physical manifestations of Henry Slade, forced him to the conclusion that these wonderful manifestations could not be explained by the ordinary laws of physics. That the tying of knots in a string, with both ends fastened and sealed and held in his and Slade's hands on the table, while the other part of the string hung under the table. Communications were written on a book slate which they had purchased, and had been sealed up by them. They heard the slate-pencil scratching like a thing of life between the slates. After giving three raps they removed the seals, opened the slate and both sides were written all over and signed. Fearing there might be something wrong they then prepared other slates of a similar kind, and when Mr. Slade put his hands on them, the pencil began to scratch, and when it rapped three times they took the same slates and carried them home and opened them, and there were other messages written to them.

Wooden rings tied together with a string and placed under the table were carried and placed around the upright part of the candle-stand, which no mortal could do without taking off the tops of the stand.

Coin was passed down through the table and fell on the slate, while the pencil passed up and entered into the box in which the money had been placed and sealed up. A candle-stand rose up and disappeared, presently it descended from the ceiling and rested upon the table around which they were sitting

A bowl of flour was placed on the floor under the table and they felt hands touching them on their legs On inspection there were the marks of hand prints in the bowl of flour and the same finger marks on their pants They were certain that Mr. Slade did not do it, as his hands rested on the table all the time, and there was no flour in them.

That hand and foot prints on prepared paper were made through the slate, though it was locked up in a box That a screen that was made of strong wood that would require a dynamic force of two hundred and ninety-eight hundred weight, or more than the combined strength of three hundred giants to rupture, was torn apart by an invisible power That lights appeared and disappeared; that it rained on them and wet their clothes in the room, and many other strange things that could not be explained by any known law of physics. These tests were through and beyond any trickery They called in the king's juggler to assist them, and he was unable to detect any fraud or trick, or make any explanation how it was done.

All of which goes to prove the apparent penetration of matter, and also of the existence of the fourth dimension, by which this invisible power can produce these strange phenomena So these learned savans of the renowned school

of Leipsic were forced to the conclusion that there was an intelligent power that could do those things which were beyond their knowledge of physical forces. That there were such things in existence that did not come within the known laws of length, breadth and thickness, which is all that we can possibly know of matter, and in these dimensions it includes all its possibilities But in the fourth dimension, says Zollner, "we have another aspect of the case; one in which our system of geometry is at fault, and its axioms cease to apply there; matter is subjected to transcendental laws and conditions are apparently reversed."

Professor Zollner, in a letter to Mr. William Crookes, who had also investigated the phenomena of Spiritualism, said: "By a strange conjunction our scientific endeavors have met in the same field of light and of a new class of physical phenomena, which proclaim to the astonished mankind, with assurance no longer doubtful, the existence of another material and intelligent world. As two solitary wanderers on high mountains joyfully greet one another at their encounter, when passing storm and clouds veil the summit to which they aspire, so I rejoice to have met you, undismayed champion, upon this new province of science. To you, also, ingratitude and scorn have been abundantly dealt out by the blind representatives of modern science and by the multitude befooled through their erroneous teachings May you be consoled by the consciousness that the undying splendor with which the names of a Newton and a Faraday have illustrated the history of English people can be obscured by nothing; not even by the political decline of this great nation; even so will your name survive in the history of culture, adding a new ornament to those with which the English nation has endowed the human race " (Transcendental Physics, page 27)

The late exhibitions of physical force by Miss Lulu Hurst throughout the United States, is enough to convince all fair-minded people that there is an invisible force, produced by the laying of her hands upon a chair that defies the strength of a dozen strong men It flung men around as though they were feathers. I found it impossible to hold an umbrella over my head while she had but one finger touching the handle. Her manager announced that she disclaimed any knowledge of the power that produced the force Her father informed me that the power was spiritual force, as he had been so informed by the spirits, but that it was not policy to so announce it from the stage, owing to the credulity of a great many people who are prejudiced against the spiritualistic theory I was satisfied as soon as I took hold of the umbrella that it was the same force that could enable my little cousin to hurl me from a chair twenty-five years ago. And here let me state, that not long since I saw the same cousin —now married and the mother of several children—and she informed me that she had long since lost that power

I know of several other mediums who have lost the power to produce manifestations, having been pursuaded by the church that it was the work of the devil My little cousin, Lillie Dobbins, was a strong physical medium, and could make a dining-room table follow her around like a dog by touching it with the tip of her finger, and make it stand on one leg and flap the folding leaves, like the wings of a bird I asked what spirit it was moving the table? It called for the alphabet, and as the letters were repeated, the name of Samson was rapped I then asked it to turn the house over. It replied, in the same way, that it might kill us. I then said, "Throw me out of the chair" and immediately I felt myself moved by an invisible force, that hurled me out without an effort

I had another cousin, Carrie Dameron, who was a rapping medium, and I tested her in every way I could, to solve the mystery It invariably rapped out the name of departed relative or friend, who would not admit that they were dead, but only passed to a higher state of existence.

One of the most peculiar tests I had occurred one night, when the negro boy, who made fires in the dwelling, being anxious to see the manifestations, had crawled under the bed, after making the fire, and unknown to any of us, but the fact of his presence was revealed by the attendant spirit rapping out the words, "Dick is under the bed." The poor boy came out affrighted, saying, "That is the devil, sure, for no one know'd I was dar"

Here let me state that that dear cousin has long since passed to the spirit land, and she often comes to me and gives me assurance that what transpired while living is more than real, and that spiritualism is true

It is evident that this is a force that has intelligence, that can come when desired and depart when not wanted, and is capable of communicating with man through raps, tipping of tables, independent slate writing and in other ways It can give names and incidents, of which no person present has any thought or knowledge While some of these communications may be erroneous, on the whole they are generally truthful; but it is not safe to place too much reliance in their knowledge of the future, for they, like mortals, are fallible, and they make many statements that are false, for they have only advanced intelligence, and many are not so wise as those living in the flesh, and it is hard to say who is at the other end communicating It may be the spirit's true name or it may be some mischievous boy's spirit or some lying spirit imposing on humanity They are there as they were here—no wiser, no better, as they depart this life, so they wake up over there in the spirit land.

Saint Paul said "We must try the spirits before we believe them" So nothing should be taken for granted, until it shall have been thoroughly tested; even then it must be taken with a great deal of allowance, for we little understand this mode of communicating Even the telegrapher requires us to repeat the message before he will stand responsible for the correctness of its transfer

This mode of communication, like telegraphing, requires time to investigate and understand We are not able to go over to the other side to compare notes and then return. We have to take it for granted that what words they send back are correct, and, so far, these statements have been of so confused and uncertain a nature that many have been led to the belief that it must be something other than the spirit of our departed friends, at best it is hard for us to understand how anything, or any intelligence can exist without a physical body, capable of making itself manifest to our five senses; yet, we hear the raps and the scratching of the pencil, but we cannot see the power that moves it

There are so many frauds and deceptions in the world that it becomes all to be very careful that they are not imposed upon. It may be a question whether it is best for ignorant masses of humanity to investigate it, as they are liable to be misled and placed under the control of evil rather than good influences, but as mankind grow wiser and better they will learn to look upon it as their future existence, and will prepare and fit themselves for that advanced stage of development. It will rob the grave of its terrors and make death only the gateway to a higher and better existence in the vast unseen universe that encompasses us. When it is understood that this planet is only a germinating world, and that our future happiness depends on how we live here, and that it has much to do in fitting us for the life to come, that is eternal; that we can not escape the burden of our own sins or shift them on the shoulders of another, it will make us more careful how we act and treat our fellow-man, for we are all brothers on the same road to the spirit land, where we will have to make reparation for all the wrongs that we have done to each other. There the law of compensation and restoration is beyond a technicality or doubt of court or jury.

CHAPTER V.

INSPIRATION AND INSPIRED MEN, SAVIORS, MEDIATORS AND MEDIUMS.

Inspiration is the natural influx of the divine truth into the human soul, and its degree is determined by character and capacity, and it is not confined to the teachings of any religious truth. Even the old Testament teaches that certain men were inspired of God to work in linen and brass and cedar and gold. Shakespeare, Angelo, Socrates and Epicteus have just as good a claim to be inspired of God as any of the Jewish prophets or writers in the old or new Testament.

All light is from the sun, whether it shines from moon or planet; whether it be reflected by brook or mirror, whether it be a stray, broken beam to prison-cell; whether it flare in the gaslight or glow in the coal of our grate, all light is first or last just so much sunlight, so all truth, of whatsoever kind or degree, is from God

" Pure inspiration is confined to no particular person, age or nation; it is as common and universal as the spirit of God. Everything that possesses life, no matter in what kingdom or stage of development, is to the same degree the recipient, exponent, prophet and beneficiary of the universal spirit of the Supreme Being Everything that moves anywhere in the illimitable territory of Nature sustains a relation more or less intimate to the spirit which animates the world. Every creature enjoys a living communion with the all-animating principle, and the relations which subsist between the little worm and the creation of worlds are just as intimate in principle as those enjoyed by man Hence, all things receive the spirit of God and bathe in it, and express it in the external in exact proportion to their capacity and absolute requirements. The human soul is a far richer soil for the growth and nurture of heavenly sentiments than any ground around Jerusalem, which may have been blessed and sanctified by the tread of Christ and the prophets "

Man's eternal organism is closely joined to the material world, but far more closely is his spiritual nature joined to that principle which enlivens and energizes the universal whole. There is nothing between man and the bending heavens. He can bare his head beneath the dome of the living temple, and there is no obstruction intervening which can shut him from a contemplation of the gorgeous creation, and if he will but bare his spirit by removing his pride, selfishness, ignorance and sensuality, which circumscribe and entomb its fair proportions, he will find nothing between him and the enjoyment of true inspiration.

The flower is truly impressed by the light and warmth of the sun, because it possesses within itself the essential qualities and properties of beauty and development, 'and hence incorpo-. rates the descending elements of vitality in its own minute structures. It is not merely a vessel for the immediate reception and impartation of light and warmth, but it receives those elements, subjects them to a chemical' analysis, and distributes the various properties to the elaboration, development and sustenance of its own particular individuality; and then in accordance with the immutable principles of distributive justice and harmony, the flower breathes forth its precious odors with which it loads the passing breeze, and thus imparts pleasure to many loving beings, while it reflects back the rays of the sun in beautiful colors that adorn Nature with their richest hues So it is with man, like every flower he is a recipient of this kind of inspiration. That is to say, the influx of thoughts, facts and principles into the soul, which that particular mind may appropriate; first to its own welfare and enlightenment and then shedding it abroad, as the sun spreads its rays over the earth for the benefit and information of those who next require the pabulum

In all ages of the world revelations of various kinds, and of different degrees of importance, have been given to mankind, through the inspiration of prophets, sages, philosophers, seers and mediums   It all comes from' the same source, it all bears the same earmarks, and it all tells us to be good and virtuous, if we wish to be happy. The Bible is full of it—beginning with Moses and the burning bush, and ending with Saint John in a trance on the Isle of Patmos   Nor was it confined to the Jews alone, but was taught to the Hindoos, Persians, and Chinese, by Brahma, Zoroaster and Confucius, long before the Jews were a nation. The writings and teachings of these men to the whole Eastern world was that sin would ultimately be abolished, that everlasting righteousness would be brought in, and that then the good deity, Ormuzd, would rejoice with joy unspeakable forever and ever, for having triumphed over his evil brother, Ahriman (the devil)

These pure men and women of all ages and nations seemed to breathe this inspiration from on high   They have spent their lives, and may have died in the cause of lifting up man from his low animal nature and pointing him to a purer and better life beyond the grave   They have been scoffed at and spat upon by those in high places, and many have been put to death; yet, afterwards they have been deified, and churches and temples have sent up their spires to honor their sainted names.

There are many men and women of modern times that have acted and been controlled by this divine influence, who, had they lived in past ages, would have been deified for their works; Luther, Calvin, Joan of Arc, the Seeress of Provost, A J Davis, and others, who have revealed many truths concerning the connection between the natural and spiritual world, and between soul and body. And there are the names of Baron d'Holbach, Charles Fourier and Emanuel Swedenborg, the Swedish philosopher and psychologist, whose writings

impress us with that inspiration. Swedenborg claimed to have seen and conversed with angels, as did Abraham and the patriarchs of old; and if there is any truth in the one, why not believe the other, for it is more recent and better authenticated.

In the writings of Plato we see the spiritual identity of man and a future life, and his philosophy reveals some very important laws of Nature, and many psychological truths, but it is mixed up with a vast amount of hereditary superstition and absurdity.   In Xenophon we find a higher degree of beauty, truth and profitableness, for no mind was ever more deeply impressed with the truths of immortality than his, because his convictions came from the gushing aspirations of the living principle within; and his philosophy contains more substantial reasons for the immortality of the soul than can be found in any portion of the old or new Testament.

Jesus Christ

Of the teachings of Jesus Christ in the new Testament, the sermon on the mount is the most sublime ever spoken by mortal man. His whole acts seem to flow from a pure heart and a refined and spiritual elevation that has caused the whole Christian world to deify him as a son of God, sent into the world to redeem sinners

In him Nature worked her best and purest material, and the influx of the divine spirit was so great that he possessed the highest development of physical and mental powers, and he stood forth a model of form, purity and goodness. But the beauty of his natural principles and the simplicity and purity of his life and its teachings have been obscured by the darkening influence of theological interpretations, which have engrafted it on Roman paganism and shrouded his life and acts in a halo of superstition, and invested him with power that he never claimed to possess   Though possessed of great healing and clairvoyant powers, he only used them for the purpose of doing good, and the many useful and beautiful moral precepts taught by him in the new Testament should cause us to regard him with deep veneration, as one of the greatest reformers of the world, and to ascribe any higher powers would be doing him injustice, for he did not profess to be a son of God in any other sense than that he was a branch on the *great-tree of hvmanity;* and he did not profess to be directed and impelled by any other spirit than the divine love, the germ of which dwells in the heart of every being, undeveloped And to this divine principle existing in others, but not so fully developed, he appealed so feelingly, in order that its qualities might advance to that degree of refinement in love and wisdom which he possessed For he was a perfect type of a man, but anything more than that tends to injure and detract from his goodness and greatness, as it is reasonable to suppose that if the birth and life of Christ had been of such a miraculous character as some wish us to believe, other profane historians than Josephus would have mentioned it, and he would have given an account of the so-called miraculous manifestations, therefore it is evident that much that has been written on this subject was the work of over-zealous or designing priestcraft

But in this age of enlightenment and reason it is full time that these vile superstitious falsehoods were swept away and Christ be allowed to stand forth in the true light of a great reformer who has founded a church that has done more to elevate down-trodden humanity than any other, therefore he stands at the head of all others as a great and good man, possessed of that divine power of looking into minds and reading the hearts of men; and, like all great and true men, willing to suffer crucifixion and death for principles that would embalm his memory in the hearts of millions to come after him, and raise mankind from an animal plane of existence to a happier and better home beyond the grave in heaven.

St Paul says that God made Jesus "a little lower than the angel," Hebrews, iii, 3 and 9, "and a little higher than Moses," " For this man was counted worthy of more glory than Moses." It is evident that St. Paul never considered Christ more than a man "full of the spirit of God." Being all good-man he was therefore a god-man, as good and god are synonyms in the old Saxon language It is evident that he was filled with the divine substance that elevates man above the low, groveling ideas of animal existence It is evident that he was

mortal and preferred to live. He died because he could not help it, and only, when betrayed, he prayed with fervor, until "his sweat was as it were great drops of blood," that the bitter cup might he removed from him He might have made himself invisible by the use of his mesmeric power over the bystanders, as he had done before when threatened with violence, as is claimed by Eastern adepts, and made his escape, but, seeing that his hour had come, he said, " Not my will but thine be done " Luke xxiv, 34

It is evident that Jesus was initiated into all their mysteries In King's "Gnostics," page 145, "there is an account of a sarcophagus, the panels of which were bas-reliefs representing the miracles of Christ, one, the resurrection of Lazarus, in which Christ appears beardless and possessed of a wand, in the guise of a *necromancer* whilst the corpse of Lazarus is swathed in bandages exactly as an Egyptian mummy " And Jesus is always represented with long, waving and curling hair parted in the middle, after the fashion of the Nazarenes

The Talmud, speaking of the " Nazaria, or Nazarenes " (who had abandoned the world like the Hindoo Yogis or hermit), " calls them a sect of physicians or wandering exorcists They went about the country, living on alms and performing cures," fasting and praying and performing miracles, like Christ and his disciples

The first Christians were, doubtless the Ebionites, and in this we follow the authority of the best critics " There can be little doubt that the author (of the *Clementine Hanilus*) was a representative of Ebionitic Gnosticism, which had once been the purest form of primitive Christianity * * * And who were the Ebionites? The pupils and followers of the early Nazarenes—the Kabalistic Gnostics who derived their doctrine from the oriental philosophy These Nazarenes were a despised sect, on account of their different religion to that of the Jews *(Codex Nazaræns)* "

Renan shows the Ebionites numbered among their sect all the surviving relatives of Jesus, and some of whom denounced him. John the Baptist was his cousin and precursor, and was the accepted savior of the Nazarenes and their prophets. They lived over and beyond the Jordan.

There is not a word in the new Testament that goes to show that Jesus was ever actually regarded by his disciples as God. Neither before or after his death did they pay him divine honors. Their relation to him was that of disciple, and "Master" was the name by which they addressed him, as did the followers of Pythagoras and Plato. He never claimed he was "God," but said he was the "son of man," the son of God meaning that *all* men were sons of God; and when he spoke to Mary Magdalen at the tomb, "Jesus saith unto her, 'Touch me not; I am not yet ascended to my father; but go to my brethren and say unto them I ascend to my father and *your Father*, and to my God and your God,'" John xx, 17, which implied on his part a desire to be considered on a perfect equality with his brethren, nothing more; that it was his astral soul or spiritual body that she beheld and that he did not wish her to touch him.

They looked upon him as a great prophet, a holy, inspired man, a vehicle used by Christos (messenger), through which the spirit of God made himself manifest to man; and in Luke iii, 22, "And the Holy Ghost (spirit) descended in a body shaped like a dove upon him, and voices came from heaven, which said, Thou art my beloved son, and in thee I am well pleased." In another place it says, "Jesus, full of sacred spirit, returned from Jordan and the spirit led him into the desert." These passages are enough of themselves to convince any unprejudiced mind that he was a great medium and seer, through whom the spirits manifested.

It is evident that Christ understood the magic art, when he says, "Go ye, therefore, and teach all nations, *. * * and lo, I am with you always, even to the end of the world," (that is, his spirit) and the apostles performed miracles in his name after he was crucified. The prison doors were opened to Peter and the jailor was affrighted. It is claimed that the keys of heaven were left with St. Peter. Baron Bronson shows that the word Patar or Peter was a mystic word which "locates both master and disciple in the circle of initiations, and connects them with the *secret* doctrines as they were taught by the hierophants of ancient

Egypt," and that the ancient "Book of the Dead," found in the tombs, dating back 4,500 years B. C., had this word written in hieroglyphics, and Jesus knew the secret meaning of the word bestowed by him on Simon, who was thereafter called Peter, whom he initiated into all the mysteries, who continued to perform miracles and wonderful things, and this power is still claimed by the Church of Rome.

Christ said, "Why callest thou me good? There is none good but *one; that is God*." "And whosoever shall speak a word against the son of man shall be forgiven him; but unto him that blasphemeth against the Holy Ghost it shall not be forgiven." Luke xxii, 10. Is this the language of a God, of the second person in the trinity who is identical with the first?

Say the Hermes, "No one of the gods, no man or lord can be good but *God* alone." Christ made use of the same expression. "To be a good man is impossible, God alone possesses this privilege," says Plato. John the Baptist did not consider Christ a god, when he baptized him (John i, 6 and 30), "This is he of whom I said, After me cometh a *man*." Speaking of himself Jesus says, "You seek to kill *me*, a *man* that hath told you the truth which I have heard of *God*." John viii, 40. And even the blind man of Jerusalem, when speaking of who had healed him, said, "A *man* that is called Jesus made clay and anointed mine eyes." John ix, 11.

Christ in all his sayings is in a Pythagorian spirit. When not verbatim repetitions, his code of ethics is purely Buddhistic; his mode of action and walk of life Essenian; and his mystical mode of expression, his parables and his ways those of an initiate, whether Grecian, Chaldean or Magian (for the "perfect," who spoke the hidden wisdom, were of the same school of Archaic learning the world over); it is difficult to escape from the logical conclusion that he belonged to the same body of initiates. Secret societies and sects extended all over the East at that time, and there is no doubt that Jesus Christ was an initiate.

The learned philologists have been able to trace this coming messiah far back in the sacred books of the ancient Hindoos, written in the Sanscrit; which is the mother language of the Aryan race. They had their trinity and they had their savior; so did the Persians and so did the ancient inhabitants of Mexico. When the latter country was invaded by Cortez, the priest said, "The devil was ahead of us; how could these people know of Christ and the Virgin Mary unless the devil had told them of it."

The Christian Adventist undoubtedly got his idea from the Hindoo, for it says in their sacred book, "When Vishnu appears for the last time he will come as a savior." According to the opinion of the Brahmans he will appear in the form of a horse, Kalki. Others claim he will be mounting it. This horse is the envelope of the evil spirit, and Vishnu will mount it, invisible to all, until he has conquered it, for the last time, then he will become visible and all mankind will become good and then comes the millenium." The Bible speaks of Christ coming again on a white horse.

The Christian virtues inculcated by Jesus in the sermon on the mount are nowhere exemplified in the Christian world. The Buddhist ascetics and Indian fakirs seem almost the only ones that inculcate and practice them, and these the Christians call heathen and send missionaries to teach them morals that they have derived from them, revamped, and under new names given to their gods, they try to teach that which they do not practice.

In the history of man, there appears to have been many saviors, who died to redeem him from sin, to teach him higher and nobler aspirations and fit him for the life to come. There are three that stand out more prominent than all the rest who have a history; they are the founders of churches that have millions of members who bow down and bless their names and through them seek to gain admission into heaven—Chrisna, Gautama Buddha and Jesus of Nazareth.

Chrisna,

The savior of the Hindoos, is the oldest. His epoch, on which European science fears to commit itself, is uncertain; but the Brahmanical calculations fix it at about 6,877 years ago. He descended of a royal family, but was brought up by shepherds. Man had, perhaps, advanced in civilization to the stage of shepherds; he is, therefore called the shepherd's god.

His birth and divine descent are kept secret

from Kansa, an incarnation of Vishnu, the second person of the trinity. Chrisna was worshiped at Mathura, on the river Jumna. (See Strabo, Arrian and Bampton.)

Chrisna is persecuted by Kansa, tyrant of Madura, but miraculously escapes. In the hope of destroying the child, the king has thousands of male innocents slaughtered. Chrisna's mother was Devaki or Devanagui, an immaculate virgin, who had given birth to eight sons before Chrisna. He is endowed with beauty, omniscience and omnipresence from the time of his birth; produces miracles, cures the lame and the blind, casts out demons, washed the feet of the Brahmans, and, descending into the lower regions, hell, liberates the dead, and returns to Vaicontha, the paradise of Vishnu. Chrisna was the god Vishnu in human form—he crushes the serpent's head.

Chrisna is unitarian. He charges the clergy with ambition and hypocrisy to their face, divulges the great secrets of the sanctuary—the unity of god and the immortality of the soul. Tradition says he fell a victim to the vengeance of the clergy. His favorite disciple, Ajuna, never deserts him to the last. There are credible traditions that he died on a cross (a tree) nailed to it with arrows. The best scholars agree that the Irish cross at Taum, erected long before the Christian era, is Asiatic. (See Round Towers, p. 296.) Chrisna ascends to Swarga and becomes Nirguna.

Chrisna stands at the head of the Brahman religion. It is spread over India and has about sixty millions of believers, who have degenerated into caste, leaving to the Brahma or the highest class, full control of all religious teaching in the vedas. And these lower caste, like the ignorant and superstitious of all countries, have degenerated or never rose to that intelligence, so they were unable to understand the symbols and sublime truths that were taught in the mythical figures of the vedas, but became worshipers of the idols that were used to represent the true religion.

Krishna or Chrisna was worshiped as an avotard of Vishnu, who was one of the sun gods of the ancient Hindoos, and by his reincarnation in Chrisna he became a redeemer, who would listen to the prayer of man; and that the gods, to execute anything for the benefit of man, he had to become incarnated in some animal or man. Vishnu, it is said, became incarnated ten times; the first time in a fish, the second time in a tortoise, the third time in a boar, and the remaining seven times were in human forms.

If we will only search for the true essence of the philosophy in both Manu and the Kabala, we will find that Vishnu is the Adam Kadmon, the expression of the universe itself; and that his incarnations are the concrete and various embodiments of the manifestations of the "Stupendous Whole." "I am the soul which exists in the hearts of all things, and I am the beginning and the middle and also the end of existing things," says Vishnu to his disciple in Baghavad-Ghita, chapter X, page 71.

"I am Alpha and Omega, the beginning and the end. * .* * I am the first and the last," says Jesus to John, in Rev. 1-6: 17. And if we will closely examine the new Testament we can see the ear-marks of the reincarnation of Chrisna in Jesus Christ, who has been made another avatar of the same reincarnation of Vishnu, the redeemer of the Hindoos.

It is thought by some of the Oriental writers that the wise men spoken of in the new Testament that came from the East, guided by the star to Bethlehem, were Brahmin priests.

Gautama Buddha.

Gautama Buddha, the savior of the Buddists, Tartars and Chinese, according to European science and the Ceylonese calculations, lived about 2,540 years ago. He was the son of a king. His first disciples were also shepherds and mendicants, and when he dies his spirit reincarnates into that of a new-born babe. His mother was Maya, or Maya deva (great Mary), married to her husband, yet an immaculate virgin. He is endowed with the same powers and performs wonders like that of Chrisna, and he also crushes the serpent's head, i. e., abolishes the Naga worship as fetishism; but, like Jesus, makes the serpent the emblem of divine wisdom. He abolishes idolatry, divulges the mysteries of the unity of God and Nirvana, and is persecuted and driven out of the country, gathers thousands of believers around him and dies with his faithful and beloved disciple and cousin, Ananda. He escaped crucifixion. At the hour of his birth there were thirty-two thousand wonders performed; the clouds were stopped in the sky, rivers ceased to flow, flowers ceased to bear, the birds remained silent and full of wonder, the animals stopped eating, the blind saw, the lame and dumb were cured, and all nature remained suspended.

He is represented in many temples as sitting under a cruciform tree, which is the "Tree of Life." In another image he is sitting on Naga, the Raga of serpents, with a cross on his breast. Buddha ascends to Nirvana (heaven), while Jesus ascends to paradise.

In the two preceding characters we can see that they are much alike to that of Jesus, and would naturally come to the conclusion that one was taken from the other, though the two former were born of royal parentage, which they forsook to become teachers of the humble and low born. That their mothers were immaculate and had holy conceptions; that the king sought to slay them; that the child was endowed with wonderful powers and great intelligence. They all performed miracles, cured the lame and the blind, cast out demons, washed their disciples' feet, descended into hell and liberated the dead.

That Chrisna and Jesus both died on the cross; one transfixed by arrows to a tree and the other was nailed to a cross; that they arose and ascended to heaven. So striking and alike are these three characters that one is forced to the conclusion that they are the same, and out of the dim rays of the past that reflect Chrisna comes the mythical outlines of the mythical Jesus, from whose teachings were drawn those of the historical Christos; for we find that under one identical garment of poetical legend lived and breathed three real human figures. The individual merit of each of them is brought out in rather stronger relief than otherwise by the same mythical coloring, for no unworthy character could have been selected for deification by the popular instinct, so unerring and just when left untrammeled.

If they were three distinct personages the similarity would impress us with the truth of the Buddhist faith: the reincarnation of the same spirit in three distinct forms, and different periods of the world's history. It may be contended that Chrisna and Buddha were characters taken from that of Jesus of Nazareth. But ample proof is at hand to show that either of these religions extends far back into the night of time beyond the birth of Christ or the beginning of the Christian era.

They all taught a spiritual religion involving about the same principles, but their followers have perverted their sublime teachings and turned them to suit their own interest, to enslave man and load his mind down with ignorance and superstition, and teach him to worship idols and symbols instead of the one living God.

The tendency in all ages has been to deify their great and good men when dead, and to make saints out of them, which has, no doubt, given rise to a multiplicity of gods and demigods, similar to those of the old Greek and Roman mythology, who at one time were men, and these sages, statesmen and warriors became the tutelar deities of their country, to whom the people made offering as a mark of reverence and to get them to use their influence in their behalf, which has tended to confuse the idea of one universal God, and to give to that God a human form, as these tutelar deities and guardian spirits and administering angels were once human beings and have evolved under the law of progress and development to higher spheres. And as they still retain their form when seen by seers, prophets and mediums, it is natural to conclude that the supreme God, the first *prime cause*, was an anthropomorphous being—a man-like god—and as the Bible says God made man in his own image, therefore man was like unto God, when in reality the Jehovah of the Jews or old Bible was only the tutelar deity of that race of people, and not the supreme God, as it is time and again said in the same book that no man had ever seen the face of God.

The three personalities, Chrisna, Gautama and Jesus, were so far above the common herd of mankind that they appeared to be true gods, each in his epoch, and they have left to humanity three religions, built upon the imperishable rock of ages, that have withstood the assaults of time and the attacks of skepticism, for man, being a religious animal, must have some God to worship, some one to pray to and do homage, and not having a conception of the sublime

truths, readily mistakes the symbols or the idols for the real person whom it is intended to represent, falls into idolatry and superstition. Thus the sublime teachings of these three great and good men have become adulterated so that it is hard to recognize them as they are now taught by their disciples and priests. But through the skill and learning of Max Muller and other philologists who have been able to trace them back to their origin in the Sanscrit language, we can see that they all had one common origin in the teachings of Christos, who is the founder of the spiritual faith of the Aryan race. "Yet," says Muller, "we find the hisry of Gautama copied word for word from the Buddhist sacred books into the golden legend, names of individuals are changed, the place of action—India—remains the same in the Christian as in the Buddhist legends."

"The sacred scriptures of Hindoo stole Brahma, the sacrificer, who is at once both sacrificer and victim;" it is Brahma, victim in his own son Chrisna, who came to die on earth for our salvation, who himself accomplishes the solemn sacrifice (of the Sarvameda), and yet it is the man Jesus as well as the man Chrisna, for both were united to their Christos; they are therefore the same, identical persons, or two reincarnations of the same spirit, which is in accordance with the Buddhist faith. The reincarnation of the Llama of Thibet, an adept of the highest order, may live indefinitely. When the mortal casket wears out he reincarnates himself (the Ego) in the body of a new-born babe, and he begins his existence in a new body. This may appear strange, yet Jesus speaks of the second birth, after the natural birth—born in the spirit. This might have reference to the will force freeing its astral soul so that it might communicate with spirits in the spirit land.

Jesus Christ tries to imbue the hearts of his audience with scorn for wordly wealth, fakir-like unconcern for mammon, love of humanity, poverty and chastity. He blesses the poor in spirit, the meek, the hungry and the thirsting after righteousness, the merciful and peacemakers, and, like Buddha, leaves but a poor chance for the proud caste to enter into the kingdom of heaven. Every word of his sermon is an echo of the essential principles of monotheistic Buddhism. The ten commandments of Buddha are found in an appendix to the Pratimoksha Sutra (Pali-Burman text) and are elaborated to their full extent, as in Matthew.

So great is the similarity of the teachings of these two great reformers that the Orientalist will not admit that they are different persons, but say that they are the teachings of Buddha. And so much alike are some of the religious services that a Portuguese Catholic missionary, who was sent to Cochin China in the sixteenth century, wrote back home saying that the devil had been ahead of him and introduced the Catholic service among them.

Apollonius of Tyana.

Apollonius of Tyana, a contemporary of Jesus of Nazareth, was, like him, a religious enthusiast and founder of a new spiritual school. He was less metaphysical and more practical, yet less tender and perfect in his nature, and he inculcated the same quintessence of spirituality and the same high moral truths. He confined himself to the society of the rich while Christ confined himself to that of the poor. He was the friend of kings and moved among the aristocracy, and he was born rich. Nevertheless they were both miracle-workers, healing the sick, raising the dead, etc., yet his miracles are more wonderful and varied and better attested. Materialism denies the fact in both cases, but history affirms it. Apollonius, who is represented as one of the sixteen saviors that mankind has had, is claimed by some to have been like Christ, crucified and rose from the dead, and appeared to his disciples, but history does not bear out the assertion.

He performed supernatural cures and, like the Spiritualist of the present day, proclaimed to the people that he was heaven-ordained. He confounded the most learned scholars of Rome and Greece. He ate no animal food, discarded woollen clothes, wore his hair long and well combed, washed his face, kept his body sweet and clean, refused to associate with women, lived single like Jesus, the Shakers and Catholic priests; was opposed to offering up sacrifices, did not think much of oral prayer, believed in free speech, taught a new religion, honor, equity, personal purity and universal education,

and performed miracles like Pythagoras, who was a bright medium and claimed to get his wonderful powers and knowledge from on high. He could perform a magnetic or psychologic cure, and was believed to be a god or a son of a god, or else a veritable Beelzebub, the prince of devils.

When Apollonius desired to hear the " small voice " (the spirits), he would wrap himself up in a fine woollen mantle, on which he stood upon both feet, after making certain magnetic passes and offering an invocation well known to the adept. Then he drew the mantle over his head and face and his translucid or astral spirit was free, which was similar to the account the Bible gives of Elijah: " When Elijah heard it he wrapped his face in his mantle and stood in the entering of the cave, and behold there came the voice."

Apollonius went to Hindostan in search of the wisdom of the Brahmins. He was brought into the presence of the chief sage of the East, who addressed him in the following language: " It is the custom of others to inquire of those who visit them who they are and for what purpose they come; but with us the first evidence of wisdom is that we are not ignorant of those who come to us." Thereupon this clairvoyant recounted to Apollonius the most notable events of his life, also his father and mother, and the incidents of his journey and who were his companions and all about him. He was awed by the knowledge they possessed and earnestly sought to be admitted into their secrets. After the usual length of waiting he became duly illuminated and returned and astonished Europe with his piercing clairvoyance and wonderful powers in healing and knowledge of the occult force.

His power of divining the future was wonderful. While lecturing at Ephesus he suddenly stopped and exclaimed, " Strike! strike the tyrant! Domitian is no more; the world is delivered of its bitterest oppressor!" At that day and hour Emperor Domitian was assassinated at Rome, and he saw it though hundreds of miles distant.

Pythagoras.

" Pythais, the mother of Pythagoras, was overshadowed by the specter or ghost of the god Apollo, who afterwards appeared to the husband and informed him of the divine origin of the child about to be born."

"Hercules, or Alcides as he was called by the Greeks, was always claimed to be the son of the god Jupiter by a human mother Alemena, the wife of a Theban king."

"Apollo, Mercury and Adonis were all claimed to be incarnations, each being 'sons of God' born of mortal woman; each being for a time incarnate on earth for the benefit of mankind; each destroyed and received up into heaven again, as mediators between the Most High Zeus, the Great Unknown and Unknowable, and sinful men."

Parkhurst, in his Greek Lexicon, says: "It is well known that by Hercules was meant the sun or solar light, and his twelve famous labors referred to his passage through the zodiacal signs." And that the Garden of the Hesperides was the Garden of Eden, and the serpent's head was crushed beneath the heel of Hercules; all of which goes to show that the ancient theology taught by Moses was the same as that which existed in India, Egypt, China, Assyria, Babylon, Persia, Arabia, Asia Minor and Palestine; with the Greeks, Romans, Celts, Gauls, modern Europeans, Australians, ancient Mexicans and Peruvians, which had its origin with the pre-historic man long before the continents took their present shape. The legends among the savage as well as the civilized man, point to the antique garb, with its shreds and patches of ever increasing theological complications, for the benefit of modern fanaticism, and the edification of those who are content to take the word of priestcraft, instead of thinking and investigating for themselves.

Esculapius.

There is a splendid description given of the great savior, Esculapius, in Ovid's Metamorphoses:

"Once as the sacred infant she surveyed,
The god was kindled in the raving maid,*
And thus she uttered her prophetic tale:
'Hail, great physician of the world, all hail!
Shall heal the nations and defraud the tomb;
Swift be thy growth, thy triumph's unconfined;
Make kingdoms thicker and increase mankind;

---

*Pythoness or sybil.

Thy daring acts shall animate the dead,
And rouse the thunder on thy guilty head;
Then shalt thou die, but from the dark abode
Shall rise victorious and be twice a god.'"

"Strabo informs us that the temples of Esculapius were constantly filled with the sick, and that tablets were hung all over the walls, describing the cures effected by *The Savior*." There is still a remarkable fragment of one of these tablets extant, and exhibited by Greuter in his collection. It was found in the ruins of a temple of Esculapius, which gives an account of two blind men restored to sight by Esculapius in the open view, and with the loud acclamations of the people acknowledging the power of the god."

Æschylus.

Of Æschylus, under the name of Prometheus, "Seneca and Hesiod say that he was nailed to an upright beam of timber, to which were affixed extended arms of wood, and this cross was situated near the Caspian Straits." "At the final exit of this god the whole frame of nature became convulsed; the earth shook, the rocks were rent, the graves were opened, and in a storm which seemed to threaten the dissolution of the universe, the solemn scene closed, and the savior gave up the ghost."

Xenophon.

There can be no doubt that Xenophon was a man of noble aspirations and a believer in the immortality of the soul. Speaking of sleep, he says: "Nothing so nearly resembles death as sleep, and nothing so strongly intimates the divinity of the soul as what passes in the mind on that occasion, for the intellectual principle in man, during this state of relaxation and freedom from external impressions, frequently looks forward into futurity and discerns events before time has yet brought them forth, a plain indication of what the power of the soul will hereafter be, when the soul shall be delivered from the restraints of its present bondage."

Cicero.

Cicero, the great orator and statesman, was also a defender of those unvarying principles that govern the universe and was endowed with a consciousness of the truth, which caused him to discard superficial theories that then shrouded the public mind in the form of heathen mythology. He was a great lover of nature, and his mind was lifted far above the herd of ignorant, superstitious humanity, which in all ages of the world is ready to put to death those noble defenders of truth and justice who teach a doctrine in opposition to that which they profess.

Cicero says: "For my own part, I feel myself transported with the most ardent impatience to join the society of my departed friends. I ardently wish, also, to visit those celestial worthies of whose honorable conduct I have heard and read much, or whose virtues I have myself commemorated in some of my writings. To this glorious assembly I am speedily advancing, and I would not turn back in my journey, even on assured condition that youth like that of Pelius should again be restored. * * * And after all, should this, my persuasion of the soul's immortality prove to be a mere delusion, it is at least a pleasing delusion, and I will cherish it to my last breath. I am well convinced, then, that my dear departed friends are so far from having ceased to live, that the state they now enjoy can alone with propriety be called life."

Socrates.

Socrates is as much, if not more, of an authority in the scientific and literary world than many of the Christian and so-called sacred writers. He testified in the midst of all his wisdom and learning to the continued presence of his dæmon or guardian angel, who warns him of danger, predicts to him events that are coming, reveals to him the state of the future life and makes the gateway of death one of glory and grandeur.

Some of the ancient writers of the church claim that Socrates, the Athenian philosopher, was a good man. As Christ was a teacher to the Jews, so Socrates was a teacher of the true philosophy to the Gentiles. "And those who lived according to the Logos," says Clemens Alexandrinus, "were really Christians, though they have been thought to be Atheists, as Socrates and Heraclitus were among the Greeks, and such as resembled them;" "for God," says Origen, "revealed these things to them and whatever things have been well spoken."

In Socrates we find those sublime truths that removed the fear of death, and in his conversations we have the best reasons ever given by man of the immortality of the soul. The manner of his death and the composure with which he swallowed the poison is only equaled by the tragic end of Jesus of Nazareth.

Zoroaster.

Zoroaster, the founder of the fire-worshipers of Persia, was born under somewhat similar circumstances to those of Christ, though his parents descended from kings. "His mother, when pregnant, saw in a vision a being glorious as Djemschid, who assailed the Deves (the Persian evil spirits) with a sacred writing, before which they fled in terror. The interpretation given by the magician was that she should be favored among women by bearing a son to whom Ormuzd (good—god) would make known his laws and who should spread them through all the East. Against this son every power of evil would be in arms." That after many trials and much persecution he should triumph, and at last should ascend to the side of Ormuzd in the highest heaven, and his foe sink into Ahrimana and hell.

King Darius sought like Herod to kill him, and on lifting up his sword to hew the child in pieces, his arm was grasped by some unseen power and was withered to the shoulder, which so frightened the king that he dropped the sword and fled in terror. They then stole the child from his mother and cast him into the flames; there he lay peacefully on his fiery couch as if in his cradle; where he was found by his mother (Dogdo), who carried him home unharmed. Many efforts were made to kill him but he always escaped unharmed. *He was placed in the way of wild bulls and wolves and fed on poisoned food, yet he escaped without injury.

At thirty years of age his mission began. He left his native home and visited the court of Iran. Being warned in a vision he turned aside into the mountains of Albordi, where he received many revelations and was lifted up into the highest heaven, where he beheld Ormuzd in all his glory encircled by a host of angels. He was there fed on food as sweet as honey, which opened his eyes so he saw all that was passing in the heavens and on the earth The darkness of the future was made to him as day, and he learned the inmost secrets of nature—the revolution of worlds, the influence of stars, the greatness of the six chief angels of God, the felicity of the beatified, and the terrible condition of the sinful. He descended into hell, and there looked on the evil one face to face. Finally he received from God the divine gospel (Zend-Avesta) and by repeating a few verses of it he would put his enemies to flight.

Celestial fire was also given him to be kept continually burning, and he at last overcame his enemies, and the king became a convert to his doctrines. Their moral teachings are pure and beautiful, and his ideal of the Divine One high and just; but in the course of centuries his followers became idolatrous and the sacred fire became more and more an object of veneration, and the sun, the loving emblem of their sacred fire, was their object of worship. They finally degenerated into what is known as fire-worshipers; licentiousness desecrated the temples and human sacrifices were at last offered This religion lasted for over twelve centuries, when it was displaced by that of the Koran, with the exception of some Parsees or sun-worshipers in India

He says, speaking of overcoming evil, "But though he has been brave in battle, killed wild beasts and fought with all manner of external evils, if he neglect to combat evil within himself, he has reason to fear that Ahriman and his deves will seize him"

Sosioch

Sosioch, the Persian savior, is also born of a virgin, and at the end of time he will come as a redeemer to regenerate the world, but he will be preceded by two prophets, who will come to announce him (see King's translation of the "Zend-Avesta" in his "Gnostics," page 9) Then comes the general resurrection, when the good will immediately enter into this happy abode—the regenerated earth—and Ahriman and his angels (the devils) and the wicked will be purified by immersion in a lake of molten metal. * * * Henceforward all will enjoy unchangeable happiness and, headed by Sosioch, ever sing the praises of the Eternal One."

The above is a perfect repetition of Vishnu in his tenth avatar, for he will throw the wicked into the infernal abodes, in which, after purifying themselves, they will be pardoned, even those devils which rebelled

"This Sosioch, or mediator, is much like the Messiah of the Jews, and here was the deep and real point of unison between the two religions, and this explains the meaning of the star which was seen in the East and which guided the magi of Zoroaster to the cradle of Christ" (See "Ten Great Religions," page 209)

Confucius

Six hundred years before the birth of Christ the Chinese philosopher Confucius, in his book "Lun-Yu," chapter V, 15, enunciated the Golden Rule: "Master consists in having an invariable correctness of heart; and in doing towards others as we would that they should do to us"

And in this noble character we find the same lofty spirit that rose above the groveling herd of humanity, whose time is absorbed in getting food to support a starving body Though he has not been deified he has left a deep impression on the morals of his people, so that he is as much an object of veneration as a savior who might have died upon a cross for a religious idea He has received the title of philosopher, a term far more appropriate than that of savior.

Mr. Kersey Graves, in his work entitled "Sixteen Crucified Saviors," says there have been at least thirty-four avatars or god-men. The following is a list:

1. Krishna or Chrisna, of Hindostan.
2. Buddha Sakia, of India
3. Salivahana, of Bermuda.
4. Zulis, also Osiris and Horus, of Egypt
5. Odin, of the Scandinavians
6. Crita, of Chaldea
7. Zoroaster and Mithra, of Persia
8. Baal and Taut, of Phoenicia.
9. Indra, of Thibet.
10. Bali, of Afghanistan.
11. Iao, of Nepaul.
12. Wittoba, of Billongonese.
13. Thammuz, of Syria
14. Atys, of Phrygia.
15. Xamotis, of Thrace.
16. Zoar, of the Bonzes.
17. Adad, of Assyria.

59

18. Deva, Tat, and others, of Siam.
19. Alcides, of Thebes.
20. Mikado, of the Sintoos.
21. Beddru, of Japan.
22. Hesus, or Esos and Bremilla, of the Druids.
23. Thor, son of Odin, of the Gauls.
24. Cadmus, of Greece.
25. Hil and Teta, of Mandaites.
26. Gentaut and Quaxalcote, of Mexico.
27. Universal Monarch, of the Sibyls.
28. Tschy, of Formosa.
29. The Logos, of Plato (The Word).
30. Holy One, of Xaca.
31. To and Tien, of China.
32. Adonis, of Greece.
33. Ixion and Quirinius, of Rome.
34. Prometheus, of Caucasus.

"Each of these saviors was born at mid-winter and their births were excited the jealousy of some kingly tyrant, and, though themselves of royal descent, were born in caves or mangers, forced to pass their infancy in obscurity and not unfrequently cause the 'massacre of all the innocents' in the district in which they are born. They are all miracle-workers, and are generally connected with some snake story, in which is represented the evil power which is adverse to them. They generally perform about the same class of miracles, preach the highest morals of the age in which they appear, and are benevolent and act the part of great reformers, and oppose the abuses of the times. They feed multitudes, cast out devils, heal the sick; finally they succumb to the powers of evil that oppose them; die a violent death, very often by crucifixion, descend to the lower regions to rescue lost souls, reascend to heaven and thenceforth become judges of the dead, mediators and redeemers of men, who offer up vicarious sacrifices to God for the sins of the people."

"These good-men or god-men," says Mr. Graves, "all appear to point to one origin in India." "How the ancient Mexican could have conceived the idea of a savior," says the priest who accompanied Cortez in his conquest of the country, "I cannot imagine unless the devil gave them the information."

So all nations have had their saviors; they make him comply with their ideal and color them black, red or white, as may chance to be the color of the race to which they belong.

"Many of the ancient statues of the god Buddha in India, have crisp, curly hair, with flat noses and thick lips; nor can it be reasonably doubted that a race of negroes formerly had pre-eminence in India." It was the opinion of Sir William Jones that a great nation of blacks (not certainly, though possibly, negroes) formerly possessed the dominion of Asia, and held the seat of empire at Sidon (more probably Babylon). These must have been the people called by Mr. Maurice, Cushites or Cuthites, described in Genesis, and the opinion that they were blacks is corroborated by the translators of the Pentateuch, who constantly render the word Cush by Ethiopia. The figures of the ancient Hindoo gods found in cave temples is very different from the present race. This points back to the remote age when all mankind were black, as is claimed by some ethnologists. The color of the first human beings was black.

To comprehend these saviors we must look upon them as great and good men who breathed the divine breath of inspiration, who by their pure lives lived in harmony with the spirit world, and drew their wisdom from the soul of the universe, which is overflowing with truth and goodness. These saviors were sensitives and were able to connect themselves with it, and to draw from it some of its secrets and divine truths.

Each wave of thought, whether of good or evil, that vibrates from the heart or mind goes out by the silent system of spiritual laws, and influences all minds within the radius of its control. The spiritual beings around us are moved and affected. It reaches out wave after wave, and is met by a response from the spiritual agencies that come down from the great central mind (God). There is no limit to the light and knowledge that is locked up in the spirit world, if man would place himself *en rapport* with it. It only requires that he should seek it earnestly; it only requires that he should trust it; it only requires that he should submit and have faith and live in harmony with nature, and do right and good will follow his earnest wishes and prayers.

CHAPTER VI.

RELIGION; ITS ORIGIN, GROWTH AND DEVELOPMENT

As the savage slowly evolved from the ape-like man, his brain became larger and more developed in the region of the moral and reflective organs. His forehead assumed a higher and broader proportion, the crown rose in the region of the organs of benevolence and veneration. Man alone has this prominence on the crown of the head, all other animals are deficient. While many animals possess a back skull largely developed, man alone has a forehead and a highly curved crown, and in the lowest there is but a slight elevation. The prominence in this region of the head is the most marked feature between the benevolent, pious and good man and the low and bad man Therefore religion is dependent on the brain development in the region of the crown of the skull.

The moral and intellectual brain was the last to evolve; as man was forced to think and reason these organs expanded and by slow degrees man became a reasoning, thinking animal. Man's religion is high or low as he recedes or approaches the lower animals, low and degraded races have a low and degraded religion, and as man ascends in the scale of intelligence his religion becomes broader and more liberal. It is the ignorant and narrow-minded that constitute the over-devout fanatic and the religious tyrant and bigot who is always a great stickler for creeds and dogmas God, creation and religion are things too broad, too high and too noble to quarrel about or to burn men, women and children because they entertain other ideas than those entertained by the orthodox believers of the time.

The most of the animals know the difference between day and night. Some know the seasons of the year; the squirrel, for instance, lays up its store of nuts for the long winter, and many birds migrate south every fall All animated nature is governed by instinct, while man is governed by reason and intuition—the latter in animals is called instinct. In man it is elevated and guided by reason What we call our first impression is this feeling of intuition that makes us religious, because it is the inner whispering of our nature that admonishes and forces us to admit that there is a future state, that the life principle never dies. Animals may have it, but they have not developed a reason or an intelligence so that they can express it, or perhaps feel it, yet they all cling to life and dread to die, they know this life but not the life to come

All strange phenomena that man cannot understand, he is ready to believe is produced by some supernatural power; it is a mystery and he is ready to ascribe it to some marvelous cause. The mind that is ignorant of these causes has a vague and indefinite idea of it; therefore he is ready to believe it is produced by some unseen being, and as he has learned from experience there are good and bad results, so is he ready to ascribe it to good or bad spirits

So by degrees he became a superstitious animal and was ready to conclude that all phenomena that he could not understand was the work of some good or evil spirit, according to the manner of its visit and its interest for good or evil This idea gave rise to good and evil spirits, gods and demons; all of which tended to create a religious feeling within his nature. As he receded from the beast this feeling was increased by the development of those organs that tended to make him a social, moral being, grateful for the blessings conferred upon him by the bountiful hand of nature, which is ever ready to assist him to rise

No other animal has a religion. It may be said to be one of the marked distinctions that place man above the brute creation. No monkeys or apes have any reverence for a supreme being. "Man is the first animal," says Professor Fowler, "that has the organ of veneration," which he places at the crown of the skull Some men have little or no reverence, and the want of this development makes them atheists and disbelievers in a supreme being and a future existence.

The moral and religious organs are the last that develop in the child, and over them the skull is last to harden Man alone possesses this craniological development, and the lower the man or the lower the race the less the brain is developed, and the harder is the infant's skull on the crown of the head, as in the case of the negro child and the inferior races and apes The phrenologist and ethnologist can almost tell the moral and intelligent status of the man by the shape of his skull and to what race of people he belongs All prehistoric skulls of man and the lower order of animals possess less brain capacity than those of more recent periods. The mammoth elephantus primogenitus of the tertiary period, though twice as large as that of the modern elephant, possessed a less brain capacity. As the world has grown older animals have grown less and their brain larger.

So religion is a matter of growth and development as well as of muscle and brain, and is dependent on the brain for its existence, so this will account for the universal idea that man has of a future state of spirits, angels and gods. As his brain increases he has a higher standard for his god. He first makes himself an image out of stone, mud or wood; then he gives it the form of a man, which is the highest conception of a form that he can conceive, and here he generally stops and becomes a man-worshiper.

It is this indwelling principle that forces up the savage to that of the civilized, moral, social and intellectual man, and as these faculties are developed man ascends and progresses, and the higher the condition on earth the higher will be his condition in spirit life, for it follows the law of progress, and as spirits progress so will man, for they are only higher beings of intelligence, and are only freed from the body, while man is the undeveloped spirit, chained to the body, only to be freed at death; therefore they act and react upon each other, and spirits attract like spirits, whether in or out of the body, so that spirits are attracted to earth and spirits of mortals ascend to the spirit spheres, when in proper condition, and this interchange is ever going on between them, ascending and descending. The spirit of the savage descends to the savage on the earth and the spirit of the savage on earth ascends to their spiritual sphere So they learn of a spirit land, and this is their religion. So it is with the Hindoo or with the Christian, and whatsoever the condition of man is on earth, he has his spiritual sphere and the spirits from that sphere communicate with him, for spirits that are not in harmony cannot mingle. "Like attracts like, whether on earth or in the spiritual world."

In this way all nations have their religion, and they get it through kindred spirits, so that Spiritualism is the origin of all religions, as it is the only way man can get a knowledge of the spirit world, for all religions are full of spiritism, and when carefully compared we are forced to admit that it has all come through the same channel, and its standard depends on the mediums and the spirits that communicate and the race to which they belonged. Some men are more progressed on earth than some spirits who have been in the spirit land thousands of years.

Religion, therefore, should be progressive; as men, spirits and angels progress, their knowledge of nature and God becomes enlarged and their intelligence becomes expanded, and so should religion become more liberal. While science has found out many of the secrets of the physical laws and benefited mankind, it has refused to look into the metaphysical laws that relate to mind, soul or spirit, and still allows man to bow down and worship the religions of Moses and Christ, who had no idea of steam or electricity, but who traveled about in dugouts or on a camel's back. What we want is a religion in keeping with the age, and the spirits demand it, for they have progressed.

Religion has its origin in the mind, like that of thought and perception. As soon as man had evolved to such a condition of intelligence that he could connect a train of thought and had language to express his ideas, he became a religious animal, and had higher aspirations than his animal desires. He looks forth into the future and believes that there is something within him that will exist forever; that he will live in the spirit long after the body has decayed and returned to the dust. This thought is peculiar to man and has tended to elevate him and force him to overcome his animal nature and aspire to reach a higher moral condition. As his moral and intellectual organs push up the front and crown of the head he becomes more humane and intelligent, he has more respect for the rights of others, and he tries to subdue his animal passions, which in time he is able to place under the control of the moral, reasoning faculties of the mind; but to arrive at that condition it costs every one a struggle. Some inherit more of the vicious animal nature than others, while it is natural for some to be good, for they are born so; but the great mass of mankind inherits so much of the animal nature that it takes a lifetime to get it under control, and it may never be done.

A Hindoo maxim says: "Brahma inscribes the destiny of every mortal on his skull, and the gods themselves cannot avert it." That is, everybody has their destiny in their skulls and if he has not the moral and intellectual nature given to him by birth, he cannot make a wise and moral man out of himself; but that he can improve himself and his condition, and his brain will develop in that direction by use; that brain grows and expands like the muscles of the legs and arms by use; that there was never a mind, however great or small, but by proper study and training might have learned more. It is a bottomless well that can never be pumped dry. The mind is a battery connected with infinity; the more perfect the battery the greater is its capacity to draw from *anima mundi* (the mind or soul of the universe), which is inexhaustible, it is a part of the deity, a spark, a divine scintilla that has gone out from the universal mind, which is called God. Therefore all well balanced minds have a high regard for truth, justice, love and virtue, and hate vice.

This love of virtue and truth struggles to elevate mankind and better the condition of all; it stands out prominently in the patriot and the philanthropist, they who in all ages of the world have struggled to overcome ignorance and prejudice. They have been defeated time and time again, but their influence is felt for ages. It will take many generations to remove the patriotic feeling of a Washington from the hearts of the American people, for all love a pure, good and patriotic man, though they may not have manhood to imitate his virtues. Still it all has its effect on society and slowly pushes up the masses from their low, animal natures and selfish desires.

When we examine the religion of the savage and that of civilized man, we see much similarity and traces of one mingled in the other.

When the Zulu sacrifices a bullock and offers up his prayer he says: "There is your bullock, ye spirit of my ancestors; I pray for healthy body that I may live comfortably, and thou treat me with mercy," (mentioning the name of his dead ancestor).

A Khond, when offering a sacrifice to the earth goddess, says: "By our castle, our flocks, our pigs and our grain, we procured a victim and offered a sacrifice; do you enrich us; let our herds be so numerous that they cannot be housed; let children so abound that the care of them shall be too much for their parents. * * * We are ignorant of what is good for us; give it to us, what is best."

The Zulu says the spirit of a dead man departs from his body and becomes an ancestral ghost. The widow will tell how the spirit of her husband came back in her sleep and upbraided her for not taking care of the children. The son will describe how his father's ghost stood before him in his dreams.

The Mandan Indian woman will talk for hours to her dead husband or child.

A Chinaman is bound to announce any family event, such as a wedding, to the spirits of his ancestors. They not only talk to the ghost of their dead kinsfolk, but offer them food.

A Russian peasant will often put crumbs of cake behind the pictures of the saints, believing that the souls of their forefathers are creeping around behind it.

The feeding of the dead is still kept up in Brittany; on All Souls' Day they will put cake and sweetmeats on the graves, and will leave fragments on the supper table all night for the souls of the dead of the family, who will come to visit them. Flowers are now left on the graves as a substitute.

John Chinaman believes, when he offers a sacrifice to his dead ancestors, of roast pig and rice, that the flavor or essence of the viands ascends and the spirit of his departed father sniffs up the odors as they rise, which pleases him and he will shower blessings down on his dutiful son, while he is at liberty to take home the cold food, the gross and material that cannot be eaten by the immortal spirit, but which is good for himself and his family to make a feast upon.

Classic literature abounds in instances where the horse and clothing were burned with the owner The burning of Patroklas with the Trojan captives and their horses and hounds, is an instance, and when he came back to the sleeping Achilles, he tried to grasp him with loving hands, but the soul, like smoke, flits away below the earth.

Hermotinos, the seer, used to go out of his body, until at last coming back from a spirit journey, found that his wife had burned his corpse on a funeral pile, and that he had to become a bodyless ghost.

Herodotus tells us about Scythian funerals, and how Melissa's ghost came back shivering because her clothes had not been burned with her.

To the present day the good wife of the Hindoo mounts the funeral pile, believing that her spirit will accompany her husband to the other world

Among the ancient Peruvians the wife of the dead prince would hang herself in order that she might continue in his service

The leading of the dead general's horse in the funeral procession had its origin in the ancient custom of killing the horse at his grave and burying it with him, so that its spirit would accompany him to the spirit world and there be his war horse. As late as in 1781, at Treves, when General Friedrich Kasimir was buried according to the rites of the Teutonic order, his war horse was killed at his grave and buried with him This custom is still kept up by the savages, and the King of Dahomey decapitates

the head of a slave when he wishes to send a message to some departed friend, and a hecatomb of wives and women are slaughtered on his grave when he dies, to accompany him to the spirit land.

Religion has its origin in the heart; it is a part of man's intuitional nature; it comes from the spiritual rather than the rational, yet it must have reason as well as faith to give it support; it must have works as well as belief, and belief cannot stand long with reason and facts. The want of positive facts, such as can be demonstrated by a scientific test, is one cause of the growth of materialism To some the test of Spiritualism is sufficient, but to others it is not. The positive materialist rejects that evidence and disturbs the subtle currents that bring those facts, which are given by a class of sensitives. Scientific minds, such as Professors Wallace, Crookes and Zollner, are able to appreciate them, but the cold materialist, like Tyndal and Spencer, reject all spiritual manifestations.

There are two classes of religious persons: one moved by love may be called *amo*, the other the *credo* The latter are interested only in creeds and forms and outward show, who are narrow-minded and fanatical and have in all ages filled the world with strife, war and dissensions. They are prompt to go to church on Sunday, when they appear very devout They may be called Sunday Christians. The *amos*, on the other hand, make religion consist of doing good, they care little about creeds and dogmas, and they try to promote peace and happiness They use their belief as a means, while the *credos* stand firm on it as a finality that is to take them to heaven.

Of the *credo* Morris says: "It is possible to be delighted with a doctrine and yet have no just conception of its practical bearings; to revel in the thought of a blessing, and yet not discern its force as a moral motive; to have an intense admiration of the principles of equity and love, and yet be a stranger to both the theory and practice of them in varied relations of life and the world."

The highest idea of a religious man is to do good and to have a regard for what is right and just between himself and his fellow man. The observance of the Golden Rule is his standard;

a just appreciation of the bountiful gifts of nature which are given to him to use and enjoy. Pleasure in every form is good in itself; it is the great allurement that God has given to his children to enjoy and not to abuse.

All wisdom and philosophy are resolved into one simple principle: that happiness and intelligence depend upon the moral development of our religious nature; without it man is but a little above a brute. An immoral genius is no genius, simply a man of talent, such as Lord Byron; but in Shakespeare and Milton we have the highest moral purity, one capable of giving a full expression of the soul.

Two men may stand on the same spot, to one everything is beautiful and lovely, while to the other it may all appear a barren waste. One looks on the bright side of the picture, while the other looks on the dark side of it. One has hope, the other despair; one is an optimist, the other a pessimist, who sees evil in everything, "that this is a vile world of sin and sorrow."

Light and heat come together in the sunbeam, and so does law with virtue of desire and deed. In becoming religious one loses nothing but often gains when least it is expected. No one can perceive its beauties unless his heart is morally good. "To know nature then, one must be true to nature. To be true to nature then, one must live looking forever to the mighty spirit who presides. Nature has been said to have an exhaustless meaning, but it is a meaning to be rightly seen and heard only by him who strives ceaselessly and prayerfully to become all that the divine image and likeness is capable of becoming, which is in fact to become humane and religious, and as we become more humane the world becomes to us more divine and man a better Christian."

Religion may be divided into two parts; that which relates to its historical forms is called comparative theology; the other is that which explains the conditions under which, in the highest or lowest form it is possible, is called theoretic theology.

Comparative theology is like that of comparative philology and can be traced back to the early races of mankind in Asia. It shows that it has taken many forms and has much to do in shaping the public mind, laws and institutions of every country, and all religions may be said to be the groundwork of every government except that of the United States, in which a new departure was taken and God and religion were left out.

There are two modes by which man gets his religious knowledge: natural and revealed. The natural is the knowledge man gets by the light of nature and reason; the revealed religion is that which comes by revelations from God, angels and spirits, and the inspiration of prophets, seers and mediums. It manifested itself to Moses in the burning bush, and he heard it on Mount Sinai. Therefore all religious knowledge we have on this subject is through revelation, and this revelation has been made to man through the mediumship of some person who has been inspired or who has held converse with angels or spirits. The record of these facts are called a Bible in the Christian religion; with the Hindoos it is called the Vedas; with the sun-worshippers the Zend-Avesta; with the Mohammedans the Koran.

"True religion is that which embraces the universe, reveals perfect *justice* to all, breathes boundless goodness, fills the reason with *light*, the affection with love, the sorrowing with *consolation*, the down-trodden with *courage*, and the despairing with the golden beams of eternal hope and happiness. It is responsive to every real human need, the infinite sources of love and wisdom perpetually flow into and flood the individual receptive spirit; and the innumerable host of the heavenly spheres freely shower their fondest affections and their most resplendent thoughts into the common life of the terrestrial millions of human beings. There is no one utterly forsaken, all are a part of the whole in the great plan of creation; no bleeding heart that either lives or dies wholly alone and unknown; there are ministering spirits and guardian angels watching over every human being; no unrequited life in this universe of love; no possible estrangement from the redemptive power of the universal presence."

All humanity moves within the orbit of the spiritual Sun according to certain and fixed laws of the spirit world. There is no gravitation equal or superior to the attraction of heaven, while our feet and our animal nature cling to the earth, yet our heads point towards the heavens. That our bodies will return to the earth from whence they came and the self, the ego, the soul, will ascend to the mansion in the skies, where it will follow the laws of progress and grow wiser, purer and better until it reaches the divine sensorium whence it came.

The supreme Power whom we reverence is the boundless and endless one—the grand "*Central Spiritual Sun*"—by whose attributes and the visible effects of whose inaudible *will* we are surrounded—the *God* of the ancients and the *God* of modern seers His nature can be studied only in the worlds called forth by his mighty *fiat* His revelation is traced with His own finger in the rocks, in imperishable figures upon the face of the cosmos, and the same forces are at work and the same laws that govern matter are now in operation as were in the days of Moses, David and Jesus Christ and the apostles It is the only infallible gospel we can recognize The earth is God's Bible, for it His is work, and He has written on the rocks characters that the geologist can read. "'Therefore," says Agassiz, "to understand God we must study His works in nature, and the more we learn of it the more we will know of Him "

The materialist says there is no God except the gray matter in our brain, yet there is an inward whispering that says "No" The ego, which lives and thinks and feels independently of us in our mortal casket, does more than believe, it *knows* that there exists a *God* in nature, for the sole and invincible Artificer of all lives in us, as we live in Him. No dogmatic faith or exact science is able to uproot that intuitional feeling inherent in man, when he has once fully realized it in himself. Human nature is like universal nature in its abhorrence of a vacuum. It feels an immortal yearning for a supreme power, without a God the cosmos would seem like a soulless corpse. Being forbidden to search for Him where alone His traces would be found, man has filled the aching void with a personal God, whom his spiritual teachers have created for him to worship out of the heathen myths.

Religion places the human soul in the presence of its highest ideal, it lifts it above the level of ordinary goodness and produces, at

least, a yearning after a higher and better life—a life in the light of God

Religion is that which distinguishes man from the animals. We do not mean the Christian or Jewish religions only, but all religions—a faculty which, in spite of sense or reason, enables man to apprehend the Infinite, under any varying disguises. For all religions have in them a spark of good Without this faculty, there could be no controlling or governing man; for all religions are nothing but the groaning of the spirit, struggling and longing after the Infinite.

This yearning after immortality has, in all ages of the world, made him a slave to priests and fanatics, to be humbugged and imposed upon, instead of being his own priest and consulting the inner prompting of his better nature He has suffered others to think for him and intercede in his behalf.

All men are mediumistic, if they would only consult and listen to their better promptings, which are ever whispering in their ears what is right and what is wrong. But, blinded by prejudice and superstition, they shut their ears to those inward whisperings, and follows the teachings of some selfish, scheming man, who, to further his ends and ambition, has, in all ages of the world, seized upon this religious sentiment in man to rule, control and govern him.

"The king is at the head of state and church The king never dies and the church never does wrong " This idea has kept the masses in slavery and ignorance They have been taught to obey and pay the priest to pray for them. The king and the priest have preyed upon their earnings, and it was to their interest to keep them in ignorance, so they could continue to prey upon them. "This unnatural and unjust religion," says Draper, "has retarded civilization a thousand years " They have used it to control man and govern him to suit their interest and not his The moment a man begins to investigate he becomes skeptical, and then he is in a fair way to learn the truth and think for himself, and worship God in accordance to the dictates of his conscience

Religion has led to endless wars that have devastated whole countries, and reduced the inhabitants to the condition of slaves, and forced them to accept the religion of some ambitious general, or fanatical priest, who had no other idea of God than that which his narrow, bigoted brain would allow him to create   So they have made gods and religions to suit their fancy, and not in accordance with the grand idea and plan of nature and creation   Said a native to a missionary

" Your soldiers seduce our women. * * * You come to rob us of our land, pillage the country and make war upon us, and you wish to force your God upon us, saying that He forbids robbery, pillage and war   You are white on one side, and black on the other, and if we were to cross the river, it would not be us that the devil would take "

Among Christians there is nothing but dissensions—a contest about creeds and ceremonies, they are intolerant and tyrannical if left to them to govern man and control his conscience   Each claims to be right and all others wrong.   Its dogmas are orthodox, but all other churches are heterodox, and are ready to go to war and cut each other's throats about something in which all may be wrong or know nothing about.

There is nothing more incomprehensible to the heathen than the trinity—Father, Son and Holy Ghost, and these three in one, all equal in the God-head—and the divinity of Christ, that he was born of a woman and still he was God   There is but one God and yet there are three, how can this be ?   Some worship the Father, some the Son, and others the virgin Mary, who was the mother.

The abstract fictions of antiquity, which for ages had filled the popular fancy with but flickering shadows and uncertain images, have in Christianity assumed the shapes of real personages and become accomplished facts   Allegory, metamorphosed, becomes sacred history, and pagan myth is taught to the people as a revealed narrative of God's intercourse with his chosen people, while thousands of books, containing as much sacred history and as strong evidence that they were written by divine hands, have been committed to the flames and their believers have been put to the torture.

The theology of Christendom has been rubbed threadbare by the investigations of science and the research of the philologist and the archæologist   It is found to be, on the whole, subversive, rather than progressive, of spirituality and good morals   Instead of expanding the rule of divine law and justice, it leaves us in doubt and dread of damnation   It fills the mind with doubt as to what course to pursue   It makes cowards of all; every one dreads death, instead of looking on it as a transition into a higher sphere and a better existence

The Jewish religion teaches us of an angry and revengeful God (which is an absurdity), who will condemn the spirits of the wicked to hell-fire and the devil, there to be roasted forever   That part of the Lord's Prayer, that says, " Lead us not into temptation," is an insult to God and common sense   The absurdity of the thought that God, the embodiment of goodness and purity, would or could, for a moment, entertain the idea of leading any mortal into temptation of any kind !   No, this part of the Lord's Prayer is directed to Satan, the tutelar genius who hardened the heart of Pharaoh, put an evil spirit in Saul, sent lying messengers to the prophets and tempted David to sin; such is the God of Israel, as described in the Bible

The various religions are like the pure white ray, broken up and scattered by the prism   Red, which represents blood, is the stronger; it has been the most prominent in all the Western religions, it has caused more wars and bloodshed than any other, while that taught by the Brahmins and the Buddhist has been like that of the blue rays; it is the slowest and it lingers 'longest in the atmosphere, which gives it the cerulean hue.   So each ray of the spectrum, by imperceptible shadings, merges into each other, and so all the great theologies that have appeared at different times, have diverged from each other until they form thousands of religious creeds and sects, when all combined represent only one *Eternal Truth.*

" Truly," says Bishop Kidder, " were a wise man to choose his religion from those who profess it, perhaps Christianity would be the last religion he would choose, for they preach one thing and practice another."   Their ministers claim to be followers of the disciples, but in no instance do they do as the disciples did, " Care not for food or raiment or gold or wealth; heal the sick or console the distressed," but always keep an eye to the good things of this earth and a fat parsonage They tell the people the days of miracles are closed, and that the door to heaven is shut, to be entered only through and by the church, that man must look to Jesus and the cross and the virgin Mary, and not to God himself It is evident that they have become degenerate and do not understand the true workings of the spirit through the occult powers that are ever ready to be invoked to assist and instruct man how to become wiser and better. In their ignorance they have deified a great medium, who understood these forces and used them to reform man and purify the church But instead of following out his directions they have used his name to mislead mankind, and they have so clouded man's intellect with dogmas that it has caused him to lose sight of his individual relation and accountability to God

The Christian religion is repulsive to the Chinese, because Jesus had so little respect for his father and mother, and his disrespect for the dead, when he said to the young man, "Let the dead bury the dead "

As a Khan said to Marco Polo: " You see the Christians are ignorant They can't get their gods to do anything, while these idolaters can get their gods to do anything that is wanted of them, insomuch, that when I sit at table the cups from the middle of the hall come to me filled with wine or other liquor, without being touched by anybody, and I drink from them I hey control storms, causing them to pass in whatever direction is indicated they should take, and do many other marvels, while, as you know, their idols speak, and give them predictions on whatever subjects are chosen, which you Christians cannot do Why should we change our religion for one that is inferior ? "

Why should the Christian sneer at the miraculous power of fakir adepts and mediums, when they only do what prophets and Christ and his apostles did—unbolt prison doors, and strike sinners blind ? Why should the devout Catholic turn from the performances of mediums and adepts, when their priest claims to do the same thing, by making the coagulated blood of a martyred saint boil and fume in a crystal bottle. A Hindoo priest can plunge an arm into the heart of his idol and out gushes a stream of blood, and he can change water into blood Indeed, there is no difference Both have the same power, both do or practice deception on the people; one is no better than the other; both are idol-worshipers, and of those mystic systems which precede by far the Brahmanism and even the primitive monotheism of ancient Chaldea

The difference between ancient and modern religion is only the difference in their civilization The Christian religion is but a similar force like all others, and equal in its line of development. Civilization is not dependent on any form of religion, but is traceable to a great variety of influences, among which that of the mingling of races is most prominent, which infuses more energy and expands the races, while freedom and science are the motive powers which the church has often crushed or retarded The leaf needs no miracle to produce a flower, nor does the child become a man through the agency of any miraculous power; it is but the result of natural growth and development

Meanwhile, we must remember the direct effects of the revealed mystery. The only way the priest of old could impress the masses with the belief in the divine power was by the performing of "miracles," by the animation of matter, by their will-power, which convinced the skeptical mind that there was an invisible power that was capable of moving matter. And to teach them that there was an omnipotent and omnipresent power, a great first cause that governed all things for a fixed purpose, with which they had an influence

The world needs no sectarian church, whether of Buddha, Jesus, Mahomet, Swedenborg, Calvin or any other. There being but one truth, man requires but one church—knowledge—the temple of God within, walled in by matter, but penetrable by any who wish to find the way. " The pure in heart see God." Nature is God's temple, and aspiration is his worship, and to understand these laws, is to make gods of ourselves, for each and every man has, within him, a spark, which, if cultivated by living a pure, good life, will always keep him in the right path, and, finally, make him a demi-god, for all angels and arch-angels have followed the law of evolution and progress, and once were dwellers in the flesh.

Man needs no savior or priest to direct him to heaven, if he will follow the inner promptings of his better nature. He will find his way, for death is as much a fixed law as that of birth, and is in harmony with the laws of nature; and the same intelligence and force that brought him into existence, will carry him through the ordeal of death, and if he has lived n harmony with these laws, he has nothing to fear, whether he be pagan or Christian.

All progress is natural, and is divine. It proceeds by laws inherent and immanent in humanity. Laws whose absoluteness affirm infinite mind, as implicated in this finite advance *up* to mind. The laws that govern this onward movement are *inspiration*—drawn from the infinite mind, whether it be pagan or Christian, whether it believes in Christ or Buddha.

The religion of the savage is not the religion of the civilized man. One is that of fear, superstition and ignorance, a fetishism; while the other should be that of science, of truth and knowledge, of reason and love. For the growing belief that the stability of law is the guarantee of universal good; or, to translate it into the language of the spirit, that law means love, is the sign of love in its practical and universal sense, is itself becoming the all-absorbing calculus, and all-analyzing prism of our spiritual astronomy—the preserver, the divine interpreter of LAW. The stoic, Aurelius, said: " Whatever happens to us is from nature, because that only can happen by nature which is suitable, and it is enough to remember that law rules all."

The world of religion is broader than Christendom has apprehended, and it is destined to widen in the sight of man as he progresses in knowledge. The opening of China to the Western nations, and their immigration and labor, are events as momentous to the religious as to the commercial and political world. India and China are full of " lights," of which the Christian has never dreamed, that have been kept in the dark and denounced as the work of sorcery and jugglery.

Let us rest assured that liberty, democracy, labor, reform, popular progress, are not empty words; they will reach beyond the assertion of exclusive rights or selfish claims into full recognition of universal duties: that liberty is not to stop in license, nor democracy in greed and aggression, nor progress to be earned through bloody retribution alone; civilization will not be retarded in its onward march by the exposure of the falsehood of any creed or church, for there is nothing can stay the hand of the *Infinite*.

CHAPTER VII

ANCESTRAL WORSHIP OF THE ANCIENT ARYANS.

The science of religion is to sift and classify it, and thus try to discover the necessary antecedents of all faith and the laws which govern the growth and decay of human religion, and the goal to which all religion tends. Whether there ever can be one perfect universal religion is a question as difficult to answer as whether there ever can be one perfect universal language.

A perfect religion, like a perfect language, is something beyond all conception All religions, like languages, must have passed through many changes. Religion is a thing of growth and development; it has its roots deep down in our spiritual nature, which are ever urging us on to a higher state, to reach out and grasp the infinite and to comprehend our creator.

The time for a belief in the supernatural in religion is past, that faith is a hallucination or an infantile disease; that all the stories told about the gods and saviors have at last been found out and exploded, that there is no possible knowledge except that which comes to us through our senses; that we must be satisfied with facts and finite things that are made manifest to us

It is our ignorance of these laws that makes us superstitious and creates a belief in the supernatural. As we advance in the light of knowledge the mysterious recedes in the darkness of ignorance.

The Archaic man supposed that every force to which his attention was directed was similar to that which he recognized in himself, and either was, or implied, a like being He was conscious, or thought he was conscious, that he (himself) consisted of a soul and a body—of something substantial and of something insub-stantial And he concluded that, in like manner, there were souls in all things He saw that there were forces in nature more powerful than he and which he could not control, and were capable of doing him good or evil, therefore they appeared to him fit objects of supplication—beings whose favor he might procure or whose wrath he might avert by offerings, prayer and supplication. Hence arose the whole system of manes-worship, and all the myths of the sun and of the moon, of the dawn, the twilight and the night; of the wind and the storm, of the earth and sea and sky.

"The uncultivated man, indeed, worshiped every force" (see "Village Communities") "that assists or obstructs him in his daily work. That worship is his recognition of the existence of such a force and of its connection, or, at least, its possible connection, with his own welfare. It was by this method he accounts for all phenomena which have attracted his attention, which his unlettered brain could not explain. In other words, mythology was the natural philosophy of the early world, and out of which has evolved the multiplicity of heathen gods and goddesses, who were special divinities to assist and direct nature, which presided over birth, life, death, dreams, trances and visions."

From these facts it was almost inevitable that the untrained intellect should come to the conclusion that the disembodied spirits bore an important part in the economy of nature. The forces that assisted him were good, those that obstructed him were bad. He was forced to acknowledge the presence of these forces, and they produced all the changes and phenomena that came under his observation, and the only way he could explain them was to ascribe them to some supernatural power.

Manes-worship, therefore, stands at the base of mythology Man sought to conciliate the spirits of their distinguished heroes and statesmen. Thus the Thebans and Athenians disputed over the body of Œdipus, and the Argives and Trojans fought for the bones of Orestes The Acanthians offered sacrifice to the gigantic Persian engineer who died in their midst, and the people of Amphipolis to the gallant Brasidas The Hindoo of the present day adores the manes of the prominent English officials who happen to be buried in their villages

So the Archaic mind was governed by a vast variety of gods, acting each on his own principles, and each seeking the exclusive interest of his worshipers. Every assembly of men had their own god and regarded that god as their exclusive property. Each nation had its peculiar tutelar deity and pantheon of gods

When primitive man had arrived at a stage of intellectual development so that he had a conception of a divine being--one greater and higher than himself—he had accomblished much. How he arrived at that conclusion the most learned differ

One of the first impulses to religion proceeded from an incipient perception of the infinite pressing upon man through the great phenomena of nature, and not from sentiments of surprise or fear, called forth by such finite things as shells, stones, bones, trees or animals; that is to say, by fetishes

Though the prehistoric and quaternary man may and did use such things, they were but rude emblems and symbols to give an expression to the belief that there was an invisible power which controlled and could render them assistance if it saw proper to so act; while others claim that it came from ancestral worship of the images of the departed dead that they saw in their dreams, whom they worked up into ghosts and spirits, who still lived in the air and could render them assistance, and that it was the natural affection of the parent that drew him near to his children, and who was ever ready to assist them in their troubles So the son looked upon his dead father as a kind of god to whom he owed his existence. In

childhood he looked up to him for protection and support, and when he had grown into manhood these ideas still lingered in his memory, and the love and affection he had for him while living ripened at his death into a feeling of reverence that is closely allied to that of veneration, so to propitiate his spirit he is led to do homage to his grave and confer on him divine rights, indeed, the ancient Aryan believed that it was necessary to make sacrifices on his father's tomb, and the Chinese still follow this kind of worship

Periodically they have a feast of the dead While the odor rises to satisfy the hunger of the departed spirits of the dead, they are practical enough to think that it does not injure the material carcass of the hog to take it home in the evening and make a feast for the mortal man While the more cultivated Aryan does not offer the viands to his dead, there still lingers the idea of strewing flowers over the graves of their departed loved ones

The Chinese bride at the present day worships in company with her husband his ancestors, so the Aryan bride thousands of years ago did homage to the gods of the house to which she was introduced, and entered into formal communion with them She was presented upon her entrance into the house with the holy fire and lustral water, and partook along with her husband in the presence of the lares of the symbolic meal She was robed in white, the emblem of purity and the robe of a priestess. She ceased to be a member of her father's house and to worship her father's gods, but became the priestess to her adopted house spirit Hence comes the modern custom of robing the bride in white, and the eating of the wedding cake and the drinking of the wine, that the ancient Aryan and his bride offered up to the house spirit of his departed ancestors.

The ancient Aryans worshiped dead ancestors long before they emigrated from the plains of Bokhara, in Central Asia, into Europe, before they had a Zeus, Jupiter or Indra. The common progenitors of our race did homage to the dwellers in the spirit world, and above all, offered their daily orisons to their own fathers upon the holy hearth and at the commencement of every meal, which was, in effect, a sacrifice. Libations and offerings were made as tokens and pledges of honor and affection to their departed ancestors, which custom still lingers in the form of saying grace before the commencement of the evening meal, while some families still set the empty chair of the deceased up to the table The spirits were not supposed to come unbidden, the offering must be made to them, their presence invited, and their share set apart. The common meal was closely connected with their family worship. Meals are an essential part of all religious worship. "The earliest religious acts seem to have been the eating of a meal prepared on an altar." (See M. De Coulange's "Ancient Cities," page 182)

They thought every object consisted of two parts of a substance and of a shadow, of a soul and of a body of something immaterial as well as of something material, that articles of food and of drink possessed this nature It was upon the immaterial part of the offerings that the spirits fed, while the earthly parts were left for man That which supported and strengthened after its kind the human body supported and strengthened by its spiritual force the spirit to whom it was presented; nor did the worshipers doubt that at every such meal their divine head sat present, though unseen, among them.

All religious festivals with the native of Australia, Africa, America, Europe and Asia, whether he be Pagan, Mohammedan, Buddhist, Brahmin, Jew or Christian, are of a spiritual nature and owe their origin to a belief of a future existence after death. The Irish wake is only the lingering custom of the ancient Celt feast to the dead

Early philosophy, then, and religion were at first one, and such a union in later times tended to produce, in the words of Lord Bacon, "a heretical religion and a fantastic philosophy." But in an early stage of mental development, the combination is one which we might expect. In their philosophical aspect these forms represented two theories the one the natural philosophy, the other the biology of our forefathers. In their religious aspect the one was the mythical, or heroic, or Olympian religion; the other was the domestic religion, the religion of the hearth, the worship of deceased ancestors. "The worship of the house-spirits," says Hearn in his work on "Aryan Households," "was a reverential religion, * * * and every meal was in effect a sacrifice, and the Aryan housefather, when he reverentially asked a blessing upon his humble abode, felt that he was not only seeking a continuance of the divine protection, but that he was securing the happiness of the spirits of his fathers and his gods "

Each household had a house-spirit which was the spirit of the deceased ancestor that still dwelt at and protected the holy hearth on which the ever-burning fire was the emblem of the comfortable element, and the origin of communication between the spirit of the departed and those living in the flesh; and it was in the olden days of our Aryan ancestors their mode of worship The husband and wife made their own offerings; he was the priest and she was the priestess, and it was the center of the spiritual life

The Aryan language contains an abundance of terms expressive of a religious sentiment of adoration, of piety, of faith, of prayer, and of sacrifice; but there is not any word suggestive of public worship—priests, idols or of temples or of altars, or that they had any middle-men who could act as go-between from God to man to forgive his sins and give him a free pass to heaven.

The house-spirits were directly charged with the preservation of the property of the household, as Horace tells us, "The guardians against thieves " "They repelled the thief," Ovid assures us in "Fasti," v 141.

He is known to the Greeks by the name of the "Hero of the House," "Man of the Household, ' by the Romans, "The Husting of the Teutons;" and "The Damovoy, or Angel in the House," of the Russian peasant of the present day. The hearth was the altar; there the holy fire ever burned, and there the gross corporeal substance of the food was purged away and its spiritual essence rendered fit for the acceptance of the spirit. On this hearth where in his lifetime he had so often sacrificed, the departed house-father received at the hands of his successor his share of every meal and heard from his lips in his own honor those words of prayer and praise

The first step in the formation of a household was marriage. Then he was a finished man, according to the Greeks, and what we call a family man. "Then only," says Menu, "is a man perfect when he consists of three persons, united: his wife, himself and his son." Our remote ancestors sought marriage for the purpose of raising a son, for it was to the son that the father could look to perpetuate the household. It was by the son, according to the teachings of Menu, that the father discharges his duty to his progenitors and by whom he attains immortality. It is the son who, in the words of Æschylus, is the savior of the hearth of his fathers. The son must be born in lawful wedlock; an illegitimate son was not only not acknowledged, but was excluded from the household.

It was of little importance what befel a man after he had raised a son. The ancient Hindoo father, after he had raised his family, left home and lived in the forest, where he might be free from care and to study and philosophize. Solon prohibited celibacy; criminal proceedings might be taken at Athens and Sparta against one who did not marry at all. Cicero says it is a part of the duty of the censors to impose a tax upon unmarried men. It was considered a crime not to get married and have no son to offer sacrifice upon his father's grave, and to inherit and keep up the household, which could not be mortgaged and sold—the land was not regarded as an asset in the way of payment of debts. The son, therefore, was the person who continued upon earth his father's existence after that father had joined the house-spirits, so when a father had begotten a son he had discharged his duty to his progenitors.

"Those animals," says Menu, "begotten by adulterers destroy, both in this world and the next, the food presented to them by such as make oblations to the gods and to the manes." The rule of the Attic law was that a bastard had no place in the worship, nor in the household, nor in the property of the parent, and it was the same in Roman, German and Norse law. A man married for duty and not for pleasure. "Mistresses," says Demosthenes, "we keep for pleasure; concubines for daily attendance upon our persons; wives to bear us legitimate children and to be faithful housekeepers." Isais said, "No man who knows he must die can have so little regard for himself as to leave his family without descendants, for then there would be no one to render him the worship due to the dead." When Leonidas selected the three hundred braves to defend Thermopylæ, he took only fathers that had sons living at home.

Cato the elder tells us that it was the first duty of the house-father on his return home, to pay devotions at the altar of the lares. See Mommsen's History of Rome, volume I, page 173.

Plato, speaking of the worship of the gods, who were only the spirits of good and great men who had progressed high in the spirit world, says, "After these gods a prudent person will celebrate the holy rites of dæmons—spirits—and after them of heroes, and after them follow the statues of the household gods, held holy according to law, and after them are the honors paid to living parents; since it is just for a person to pay to living parents; since it is just for a person who owes the first and the greatest of debts to pay those that are of the longest standing, and to think that all the things he has acquired and holds he owes to those who begot him and brought him up, for supplying what is required for their service to the utmost of his power, bringing from his substance first, and in the second place from his body, and third from his soul, by paying off the debts for their care of him, and in the favor of those who gave the pangs of labor as a loan to the young, and by returning what has been due a long time to those who in old age are greatly in want. It is requisite, likewise, to hold preeminently a kind language towards his parents, because there is for light and wicked words of punishment most heavy, for Nemesis, the messenger of justice, has been appointed an inspector over all persons in matters of this kind."

"For as something is always flowing away from us, it is necessary for something, on the contrary, to be flowing to us. Now recollection is the influx of thoughts which had left us. * * * Each person while his dæmon (spirit) is standing steadily, going on successfully or unsuccessfully to places as high and steep, while dæmons (spirits) are opposing with certain disturbances; and that it is meet ever to hope that the deity will, when troubled, fall upon the good state which he has given, makes them less instead of greater and causes a change from the present state to a better one with respect to the good things, the contraries of these, that they will always be present to them with good fortune." Plato, volume V, page 161.

The respect for another's property was due to the respect or fear for the spirits that guarded that property. It is still a custom among the nomads of Central Asia if a horse is stolen for the owner to go to the grave of the father of the suspected horse thief and stick a spear into the grave. This proceeding is understood by the thief to be a complaint made to his deceased house-father's spirit, and if the suspicion be well founded the horse is found the next morning tied to the spear.

Word, in his book, "Journey to the Source of Oxus," gives an instance where the grain was piled up around a graveyard. He inquired of a chief, Agha Maheide, the cause. "The old man put the forefinger of his right hand to his lips and looking at me said, 'God forbid; bad as men are they will not pilfer in the presence of the dead.'" The natives prefer to trust their valuables to the sacred guardianship of such a place rather than to a weak and failing brother.

There are many people who will not desecrate a graveyard, and who believe that the spirit will avenge the wrongs done to it when in the flesh. Mr. Taylor, in his book, "Primitive Culture," gives an instance of where a Brahmin cut off the head of his mother, with her consent and request, so that her spirit might punish a neighbor who had repudiated some small debt which he owed to the household. The remarkable custom of setting *dharna*, which once existed in Ireland, and of late years has been prohibited by the penal code in India, traces of which, perhaps, may be found in the Twelve Tables. The religious sentiment of the Archaic society of the Aryan race was a force which recognized property in the household which was guarded by the house spirits.

The Chinese still carry the bones of the dead back to China to be interred. Such worship was natural, according to the Archaic ideas; but far more natural, by the same standard, was the belief that the spirits of those whom men loved and honored in their life, continued after death their vigilance and their aid. The interests of men in the flesh were also their interests in the spirit, and the lives and the hates of this world followed the deceased to that world which lay beyond the grave. Manes-worship, therefore, stands on the same base as the more picturesque worship of Olympus. Thus primitive worship and that great train of consequences that has been transmitted to us, depends, like primitive mythology, upon the state of our intelligence. It is, after all, the intellect that ultimately directs and determines the main current of the varying and tortuous stream of the world's history.

"The Locan gods," says Mr. Taylor in his "Primitive Culture," volume II, page 110, "the patron gods of particular ranks and crafts, the gods from whom men sought special help in special needs, were too near and dear to the inmost heart of pre-Christian Europe to be done away without substitutes, so they substituted saints who could answer their prayers. Some have St. Cecilia, the patroness of music; St. Luke, patron of painters; St. Peter, of fishmongers; St. Valentine, of lovers; St. Sebastian, of archers; St. Crispin, of cobblers; St. Hubert, who cures the bite of mad dogs; St. Vitus, of vitus dance; and St. Fiacre, of the hackney coaches.

As a rule every trade, every profession, every guild, every tribe, every clan is also a caste, and the members of a caste not only have their own special objects of worship, but the principal deities likewise. So in the nineteenth century we still have St. Valentine's day on the fourteenth day of February for making merry. On this day it was supposed by the ancients the birds of the air made choice of their mates, and that it was a favorite day with this merry goddess to be around and aid the boys and girls in their courtships.

There is no evidence that the Aryans were a polytheistic people. Pictet is of the opinion that their original belief was one true God, while Hearn in his work, "Aryan Households," thinks that the polytheistic pantheon was not of a religious origin, but only scientific, and was designed merely to explain in the rude fashion of an early time the ordinary phenomena of nature. They had a word which corresponded with that of Vesta, which goes to prove that the Aryans recognized the hearth. It does not indicate how far in their eyes the hearth was holy

The Hindoo, Greek and Roman pantheons had their origin not so much as distinctive religions, as they were a professional class or a literary clan

The magi of the ancient Persians, the Brahmins, the Hierophants of ancient Egypt, and the Levites of the Jews, were all a privileged caste, and used their knowledge to control their ignorant masses through their religious feelings and dread of a future punishment or in hope of a reward for doing good So they manufactured gods to suit their wants, and these gods made such revelations as suited the interest and wishes of this favored class

Gladstone said, "that the pagan deities represented deified men Honest gods were heroes deified a little above mortal man, invested with passions of love and hate, courage and cowardice, united with noble sentiments, base and vulgar thoughts, with lofty and sublime ideas, all wrought up by fancy so as to work upon the minds of the people "

It is the opinion of Herbert Spencer that "the rudimentary form of all religion is the propitiation of dead ancestors, who are supposed to be still existing and to be capable of working good or evil to their descendants." In order to better propitiate the favor of his dead ancestor he sometimes carves his image in wood or stone, which sentiment in time lapses into idolatry. Every object which strikes the rude fancy as analagous to the character of an individual may become an object of worship. The savage molds his deity according to the caliber of his mind, out of mud or carved from wood or stone.

Deep down in the human breast is implanted a religious belief that behind all visible appearances is an invisible power; underlying all conception is an instinct or intuition from which there is no escape; that beyond material actualities potential agencies are at work, and through all belief, from the stupid fetishism to the most

exalted monotheism as a part of these instinctive convictions, it is held that there is a being (or beings) who rules man's destiny, and that it may be propitiated, to which all turn their eyes and lift up their prayers when in distress and danger, that cannot be averted by the power of man.

The word mythology is derived from *mythos*, fable, and *logos*, speech. It relates to the genesis of gods and their nature It is a mass of fragmentary truth mixed up with fiction, built up of dead facts cemented with wild fancies It is the effort of the untutored man to explain the origin of things In the black clouds he sees evil, in the flowing brook, in the rustling branches he feels the breathing of gods, goblins dance in the twilight and demons howl in the darkness of night. When evil comes God is angry, when fortune smiles God is pleased

"Myths," says Bancroft in his "Native Races," volume III, page 16, "were the oracles of our savage ancestors, their creeds, the rule of their life, prized by them as men now prize their faith, and by whatever savage philosophy these strange conceits were eliminated, their effect upon the popular mind was vital Anaxagoras, Socrates, Protagoras and Epicurus well knew and boldly proclaimed that the gods of Grecians were disreputable characters, not the kind of deities to make and govern worlds."

"Everywhere," says Herbert Spencer, "we find expressed or implied the belief that each person is double; that when he dies his other self, whether remaining near at hand or gone far away, may return and continue capable of injuring his enemies and aiding his friends." This idea of duality, he is of the opinion, had its origin with the savage, whose image is reflected in the brook, or his shadow which follows him everywhere, moving as he moves In the dream the images are as perfect as in life, and this has led man to believe in the existence of a spiritual body.

All religion believes in prayers and sacrifices, and there has never been found a race of human beings but they had some kind of religion. Says Max Muller, in his lectures on "The Growth of Religion," "it is an inherent characteristic of man." The Fiji believes the shooting stars are gods and the small ones the departing souls of men. The Benin negroes regard shadows as their souls. The Maori word *mota*, a soul, meant a shadow, while the idea of God being everywhere sprang from a spirit, and the idea of a spirit from that of a shadow.

Tacitus informs us that the ancient Germans count those only as gods whom they can perceive, and by whose gifts they are clearly benefited, such as the moon, sun and fire. The savage has no fixed ideas about religion; he has no bible or catechism, only some sacred songs and customs taught to him by his mother. His religion floats in the air, and each man takes as much or as little of it as he likes.

A negro was worshiping a tree, supposed to be his fetish, with an offering of food, when an European asked him whether he thought that the tree could eat. The negro replied, "Oh, the tree is not the fetish; the fetish is a spirit and is invisible, but he has descended into the tree. Certainly he cannot devour our bodily food, but he enjoys its spiritual part and leaves behind the bodily part, which we see."

The stone on which all the kings of England have been crowned is an old fetish, and the coronation of Queen Victoria is only a survival of an old Anglo-Saxon fetishism. So is the counting of the beads in the rosary, or kissing the cross, an act of fetishism. Portuguese sailors fasten the image of St. Anthony to the bowsprit of the ship, and kneeling, address it in the following words: "St. Anthony, be pleased to stay there till thou hast given us a fair wind for our voyage." A Spanish captain tied a small image of the Virgin Mary to the mast of his ship and declared that it shall hang there until a favorable wind is granted him. This is his fetish.

Every religion is a compromise between the wise and the foolish, the old and the new, and the higher the human mind soars in its search after divine ideals, the more it becomes necessary to have symbols to convey to the untutored mind of the childlike majority of people who are not capable of realizing sublime and subtle abstractions. Therefore they worship the thing rather than what it was intended to represent. While we laugh at the fetish worship of the negro, if we would only look around in our own churches we would see many fetish objects or idols. The Portuguese sailor saw the poor negro fetish and made fun of it, yet he wore around his neck a like fetish in the form of a cross. So there is no religion entirely free from fetishism; nor is there any religion which consists entirely of fetishism, for back of all religion there is a spirit in some form which relates to the great creative cause.

When religions were founded nothing was known of science, of astronomy, of geology, or of the universe. The earth was the great center around which the sun, moon and stars rose and set, like little lamps hung up in the heavenly vaults to light up the firmament. The invention of the telescope by Galileo in 1610, startled the religious world. The Roman Church saw that it would lead to new discoveries in astronomy which would shake the foundation and then throw down the edifices of their religion, which was based upon the bible and the stability of the earth, the littleness of the sun, moon and stars. The church burned in effigy Pierre d'Albano, the author of a work on astronomy, in 1327, and in the same year burned Cecco d'Astoli, of Florence, for proclaiming that the earth moved. In 1600 the church burned Brieno at Rome, for professing the same belief, and imprisoned Campanella for twenty-five years because he assented to the philosophy of Galileo. They made Galileo retract in 1630. It put a close guard on the words of Ciampoli in 1615, and in 1625 it burned Antonio de Domines, and no one dared to express the idea that the earth was round or that it revolved around the sun. Copernicus dared not publish his work until his death. Kepler, the legislator of the skies, a Protestant, dared not quit England and was persecuted by the church and accused of heresy. His aunt was burned for sorcery at Weil. His mother was accused of sorcery and imprisoned at Stuttgardt in 1615. Roger Bacon, a learned friar of Oxford, was thrown into prison because he studied physics and astronomy and taught magic.

In France the illustrious Descartes was a wanderer and an exile through life. He was pursued everywhere by the hate of bigots. He was a scientist and an astronomer, and for that reason was deemed an enemy to the church and to God. A learned Jesuit, Fabri, was imprisoned in Rome for saying, in a sermon, that "the motion of the earth once demonstrated, the church must interpret in a figurative sense those passages of the scripture that are opposed to that principle." For they inserted Joshua commanding the sun to stand still, as it was so written in the word of God, the bible.

To-day mankind is governed by reason, and the ancient religions must be ignored, for they are founded on blind faith in what they are told. The idea of this earth being the center of all objective nature, when in reality it is only one of the particles; a grain of sand in the vast oceans of worlds that are spread out through the skies. Far from affirming that everything was made for man, it should be proclaimed that the universe is a continuous whole, an unbroken chain, of which mankind is but a link; and that he, like all other things, must move on to a higher state of existence; that there is no retrogression; that on and upward is the watchword of all nature, which is moved by the laws of evolution and progress, which is now an admitted fact by the more intelligent thinkers.

The religion of the twentieth century must be a religion of science and not repulsive to reason. While old religions have grown great in blood and tears, by persecutions and torments, amid the suffering of martyrs and cruel expressions of the adherents to old doctrines, the religion of the future must be prepared by the unanimous consent, by universal conversion, which will rise without the cost of a tear or a drop of blood. It will be founded on reason and justice, and will spread over the whole earth as fast as science can beat back ignorance and superstition. Steam, electricity and the printing press are now doing the work and laying the foundation of the future religion.

"Religion may transcend phenomena and rise to a region which mortal science may not enter; indeed, it must do so; the more it ascends to the height of its great argument, the more it expands and draws nearer to the infinite; but if it have no basis than emotions, and reject all that intuition, science and reason may offer for its justification, it may not soar to that ' purer ether, that diviner air,' where faith is merged in knowledge." According to

Quatrefages, "religion is a belief in beings' superior to man, and capable of exercising good or evil influence upon his destiny; and the conviction that the existence of man is not limited to the present life, but that there remains for him a future beyond the grave." True reason and religion have an eye for earth as well as heaven. Like the tall sequoia of California, their branches are in the sky, but their roots are deeply imbedded in the earth.

So it is necessary to look to the physical wants of man as well as his spiritual nature; a man can be a better Christian on a full stomach than on an empty one. It is just as necessary to send to the heathen the plow and the schoolmaster as it is to send the bible and the minister.

All religions are good and worthy of respect, because they enable us to render to God the homage of grateful and submissive hearts. It brings man into communion with the divine mind, and by prayer we link ourselves with Him; it elevates us and lifts us up to the immortal; it makes us better, whether God hears our prayer or not, and we know and feel that it makes us better.

But the doctrine of a religion is another thing, one that cannot bear or endure the scrutiny of reason. The doctrine of the Buddhist, which restricts human life to the earthly existence, which denies personal immortality to man, absorbing the individual at his death into the bosom of the Great All, in Nirvana, is revolting pantheism. The doctrine of Mohammedanism, which has no basis but the words of its founder, gathered under the title of Koran, and regarded as a divine revelation, is not taken in earnest by the Mussulmen themselves, but held as a kind of political power which they enforce with the sword and torch. The doctrine of Judaism, which rests on the advent, always vainly expecting a savior, a messiah, who never comes, the need of whom is in no wise apparent, is almost ridiculous and absurd.

The doctrine of original sin, which lies at the foundation of Christianity, is illogical and unjust. To hold all mankind—the past, present and future—responsible for the indiscretion of Eve for eating an apple that was placed on a tree to tempt her, an event supposed to have occurred some six thousand years ago in an obscure corner of Asia, and that, to atone for this original sin, besides being driven out of the Garden of Eden, which science has shown to be a myth, God had to send His only son Jesus to be crucified between two thieves, to ransom all men, condemned and lost in consequence of the indiscretion of Adam and Eve, who did a good thing by eating the apple that opened their eyes to their ignorance and nakedness, is contrary to all reason and common sense.

No one can be honest with himself and say that his religious views have never changed from childhood to old age. The older we grow the more we learn to understand the wisdom of a childlike faith, when we are ready to believe anything our parents teach us, until we have advanced and learned to think and act for ourselves. So the idea of God in childhood is different from that of manhood, and that idea of religion changes with our intellectual development. No two persons have and entertain the exact ideas of a religious belief. So all religion should be progressive and in full accord with the prevailing ideas of science and the knowledge of things. The religion of the ancient Hindoo, Egyptian, Greek, Roman or Hebrew is not suited to our present state of civilization and enlightenment. A religion that is not able to grow and live with us as we grow and live, is dead and will not admit of progress. A religion that is definite and unvarying in its uniformity, so far from being a sign of honesty and life is always a sign of dishonesty and death. Every religion that is to be a bond of union between the wise and foolish, the old and the young, must be pliant, must be high and deep and broad, bearing all things, believing all things, possessing all things, and enduring all things. The more it is so, the greater its vitality, the greater its strength and the warmer its embrace.

If religion refuses to accompany science it will be left alone: scientific truths are only destructive to that which opposes them. A religion which is not contradictory to the laws of nature has nothing to fear from science, and will progress hand in hand with it. While seience is limited in research by laws which govern matter, that of the spiritual relates to the intelligence that directs to the fountain from which all knowledge flows.

CHAPTER VIII.

The Greeks were truly a mediumistic race of people; they were great lovers of the beautiful and lived close to nature, and followed her laws and took their models from her, and in so following her they succeeded in rising to an elegance of refinement and a perfection of beauty that has never been excelled Her poets, orators, statesmen, warriors, philosophers, painters and sculptors are the masters of all ages, whom all try to emulate but none claim to excel

Her religion was natural, and her gods and goddesses were only progressed human beings who had cast off the outer coil, and had become more perfect, wiser and better, but who still retained mortal feelings and passions, that made them still linger and take a deep interest in the affairs of mortal man

The Greek religion differs from all the other religions in this the human character of its gods. The gods of Greece are men and women idolized and on a large scale, but still they are intensely human and but little above mortals The gods of India were vast abstractions and, as they appear in sculpture, are hideous and grotesque idols The gods of Egypt seem to pass away into mere symbols and intellectual generalizations, but the gods of Greece are persons, warm with life, radiant with love and beauty, having their human adventures, wars and love scrapes The symbolical meaning of each god disappears in his personal character They were not confined to any particular sphere, but like mortals mingled together, having different interests and occupations, like a number of human beings, young, healthy, wise and beautiful and endowed with immortality.

They are not trying to save souls by any ascetic means, no intention or bother about making progress through the universe by obeying the laws of nature, but were bent on pleasure, on having a good time. Fighting, feasting and making love were their usual occupations If it can be said they cared for governing the world, it was in a loose sort of a way, with no regular system or laws They interfered with human affairs only from time to time as it suited their whim or passion They announced no moral law, and they gave no precept or example to guide men's consciences.

According to the Jewish religion man was made in the image of God, but according to the Greek religion the gods were made in the image of man Heraclitus says, "Men are mortal gods and the gods immortal men" The Greeks, like the modern 'Spiritualist, believed that the gods were close to him and in his midst, on the summit of the mountain, among the clouds, often mingling in disguise, and they made themselves visible or invisible at their option They were only advanced Greeks, a little higher, but not very much wiser or better. They beheld themselves reflected in their deities, and they conjectured themselves up in the heavens, and saw with pleasure a race of divine Greeks in the skies above, corresponding with the race of Greeks below.

The Greek religion, like that of modern Spiritualism, was delicious and calculated to make men happy and take away the fear of death It was without austerity, asceticism or terror; a religion filled with forms of beauty and nobleness, kindred to their own, with gods who were capricious, indeed, but never stern,

78

and seldom jealous or cruel. It was a heaven peopled with such a variety of noble forms that they could choose from among them as their protector the one whom they liked best, and possibly themselves be selected as favorites. Each person had his guardian deity or spirit; the hunter, on a moonlight night, might chance to behold the graceful figure of Diana gliding through the woods in pursuit of game, while the happy inhabitants of Cyprus might come suddenly on the fair form of Venus resting in a laurel grove. The Dryads could be seen glancing among the trees, and the Oriads heard shouting in the mountains, and the Naiads found asleep by the side of their streams. If the Greek chose to do so he might take his gods as the subject for a poem, the model for a statue or a picture.

The Greek religion did not guide or restrain, it only stimulated man. Nowhere on earth, before or since, has the human being been educated into such a wonderful state of perfection or such an entire and perfect unfoldment of itself as in ancient Greece. There every human tendency and faculty of soul and body opened into symmetrical proportions. That small country, not larger than the State of Maine, carried to perfection in a few centuries every human art.

Everything in Greece was artistic, because everything was finished, was done perfectly. On that little peninsula ripened the masterpieces of epic, tragic, comic, lyric and didactic poetry; the perfection in every school of philosophy, history, oratory, mathematics, sculpture and painting. She developed every form of government and gave us our model for a republic, and she fought and won the great battle of the world. Before her time everything in human literature and art were rude and imperfect attempts; since then everything has been a rude and imperfect imitation, and it was all owing, in a great measure, to her liberal spiritual religion.

The gods of the Greeks were men and women; they were not abstract ideas, concealing natural powers and laws. They were open as sunshine, bright as the moon, and a fair companion of men and women, idolized and gracious; just a little way off, just a little way up in the air. It was humanity projected up into the skies, a divine creature of more than mortal beauty, but thrilling with human life and human sympathies.

They had gods and goddesses, muses, fates and furies without number. Every woodland, lake and stream had its nymphs. Mount Olympus swarmed with them; here they assembled and discussed the affairs of nations and men. They had Jupiter or Jove, the supreme god, and Juno, his wife, who sometimes took offense at her husband, for his flirtations with the other goddesses and sometimes with a beautiful mortal maid. His attendants were the beautiful Hebe and Ganymede. They had a brave Mars, the god of war; the wise Minerva, who sprang from the brain of Jove, and who espoused the cause of Troy; the beautiful Venus, that came from the sea-foam, typical of the fact that life first had its origin in the sea. She warmed the hearts of men with love, and her mischievous boy, Cupid, was always shooting arrows into the hearts of the unsuspecting youths, and for a joke he would let a stray arrow fly at the heart of some old bachelor or widower that would send him around among the fair maids in search of a wife. And there was Diana, the goddess of hunting, with her fleet greyhounds, to whom all the sporting fraternity paid reverence; and the wing-heeled Mercury, who flew through the air to carry messages from one god to the other.

They were all live gods and goddesses and endowed with passions like mortals. They were only a little above man and were invested with the power of going where they wished unseen and under no restraint to mortal man; indeed, they were only the spirits of mortals, for they claimed that they all had been men and women once, but had cast off the mortal coil and assumed the robes of immortal gods. Even when great men died they were often deified and called gods or demi-gods.

Such a religion was calculated to make a people brave and polite and to inspire them with a love for the beautiful and grand. With the belief that these were gods and goddesses, ever ready to commend them in that which was good, noble and brave, and condemn them in cowardice and infidelity to state, and who took an interest in their welfare and rejoiced in their valor and success at arms. "To-night," said Leonidas to the three hundred brave Spartans at Thermopylæ, "we shall sup with the immortal gods!" "On! sons of the Greeks!" was the battle-cry of Marathon; "above you the spirits of your fathers watch the blows which, to preserve their tombs from desecration, you strike to-day."

It was this belief in immortality that inspired Homer to write the great heroic poem that in time became the bible of the Greeks. The gods and goddesses therein pictured are nothing but tutelary deities that had espoused the cause of certain men and nations. They were nothing but patron saints that had ascended to the spirit land, yet they still lingered around their favorite abodes and took an interest in mortals.

"The gods," says Homer in XVII Odyssey, page 475, "like strangers from some foreign land, assuming different forms, wander through cities, watching the justice and injustice of man. There were avenging demons and furies who haunt the ill-disposed, as there are gods who are the protectors of the poor."

In the twentieth book, Homer puts into the mouth of Achilles, after the death of his beloved Patrocles, these words:

"'Tis true, 'tis certain, man, though dead, retains
        tains
Part of himself; the immortal mind remains;
The form subsists without a body's aid,
Aerial semblance and empty shade.

"This night my friend, so late in battle lost,
Stood at my side, a pensive, plaintive ghost;
Even now familiar, as in life he came,
Alas! how different! yet how like the same."

The fiery imagination and the subtle and vigorous intellect of the Greeks peculiarly fitted them for the reception of the impressions from the spiritual, invisible world, as we see in the writings of Homer, Æschylus, Sophocles, Xenophon and others. The following is an extract from Hesiod:

"Invisible the gods are ever nigh,
Pass through the mist and bend the all-seeing
        eye;
The men who grind the poor, who wrest the
        right,

Awless of heaven's revenge, stand naked to
        their sight,
For thrice ten thousand holy demons rove
This breathing world, the delegates of Jove;
Guardians of men, their glance alike surveys
The upright judgments and the unrighteous
        ways."

The Greeks saw gods everywhere; the eternal snows of Parnassus, the marble temples of Athens glistening in the sun, the thousand isles nestling in the Ægean sea, the fragrant groves where the philosophers disputed, the fountains shadowed by plane trees, the solemn fields of Platæa and Marathon; each and all of these had their attendant spirits. A thousand deities received homage in a thousand temples, and for fear they might have offended some one of the many gods, they erected one to the "Unknown God." "That one," St. Paul said, "that he worshiped." The Greeks believed that the spirits controlled the destinies of men and nations, and took part in their affairs; were ever present, though everywhere unseen; knowing all things yet known to none; eternal, invisible and incomprehensible. Gods who mingled visibly in the actions of men, who clothed themselves with material forms and lead them on to victory; who shared the passions of humanity and sympathized with their infirmities, who controlled the present and gave omens of the future, were the beings that the Greeks loved or feared, and bowed down to to do homage and erect temples.

Their poetry is full of sublimity, representing one god as appearing in the clouds and hurling down thunderbolts into the midst of the contending armies of earth. At times the gods get angry and take sides in the affairs of men, as in the case of the siege of Troy. A god is often represented as wandering through the country in the form of a beardless youth, challenging men to play with him on the lyre. A goddess snatches from out the midst of battle an endangered warrior, whose noble form she has become enamored of, and thus saves his life by enveloping him in a mist and removing him from sight. Another goddess, mounted on her celestial steed, rushing through the air from capital to capital, arousing surrounding nations to take up arms in the defense of some common cause that she has espoused. They filled the earth and skies with beings of interest, and made life a romance, and it was a pleasure to die in the defense of country and the right. It infused into the heart a love of country, bravery and devotion that has never been equaled, a refinement and a culture that has never been excelled, and a faultless physique and loveliness and beauty that has in all ages of the world been the model of every artist and the pride of every master to imitate.

They worshiped the beautiful, and her artists and painters strove to make their pictures and statues perfect. Through this beautiful mythology constantly breaks the radiance of the spiritual world, which informs us that these myths are only the representatives of beings in the spirit land that take an interest in the affairs of man, but were so clouded in mystic lore that they were taken for heathen rites—an abominable absurdity—until its true meaning was interpreted in the light of modern Spiritualism, and proven that these gods and goddesses were merely progressed human beings in a higher state of development.

The Greeks had their mediums through whom they communicated with the different tutelary gods and goddesses, patron saints and spirits. They never went to war or did any important act without consulting their oracles, and their wonderful predictions, according to the historians have been fulfilled. The most renowned of the oracles was at Delphi, where the Pythoness, a priestess or medium, sat upon a tripod over a fissure in the rocks, from which arose a vapor that had an inspiring effect on the medium. Soon she would go into a trance, like some of our modern mediums, and then, generally in poetry or doggerel verse, she would utter some statement of a prophetic nature, which would run about as follows:

"See I number the sands; I fathom the depths
    of the oceans—

Hear even the dumb; comprehend, too, the
    thoughts of the silent;

Now, perceive I am an odor, an odor it seemeth of lambs' flesh;

As boiling it seemeth, commixed with the flesh
    of a tortoise;

Brass is beneath and with brass is it covered."

This was given in response to a question of Crœsus, of Lydia, who had sent an embassador to Delphi to test its truthfulness. He had at that hour gone into the kitchen of his palace and cut in pieces a lamb and a tortoise, and placed it in a brass vessel and covered it with a brass cover and commenced to cook it. This was a satisfactory test, so he sent back his embassador with three thousand oxen, numerous gold and silver vessels, a gold lion, one hundred and seventy ingots of the same metal, with a girdle and a necklace of incredible value. Depositing them before the shrine of the goddess, the embassador of Crœsus demanded whether he should go to war against the Persians. The oracle replied, "When a mule becomes the ruler of the Persian people, then, O tender-footed Lydian, flee to the rocky banks of Hermos, make no halt, and care not to blush for thy cowardice." This Crœsus misunderstood, not aware that Cyprus was the son of a Median princess and a Persian of humble condition, and was the ruler prefigured under the type of the *mule* king. He made war upon the Persians and soon he was forced to flee, as the oracle had predicted.

These oracles became the recipient of vast gifts from kings and rich people that consulted them, and they were consulted by a far greater number of people than now-a-days consult our mediums; while then, as now, they made many mistakes, and there were impostors then as now, who humbugged and imposed upon the credulous. The belief in their predictions was then universal, and no general would go to war without consulting them. Even Alexander the Great consulted the oracle at Delphi, but the medium said that she was not ready; the spirit did not move her. Alexander took her by the arm and said she must give him a sitting. While leading her to the tripod, she said, "Alexander, thou art irresistible." He at once let her go and started off. She called him back, and said that she did not mean that, but to wait, she had something more to say. "No," said Alexander, "that is enough." He immediately returned to his army and told them what the oracle had said, "that he was irresistible," and it was the battle-cry of the army which ever lead his cohorts to victory. He was warned by the magi not to enter Babylon, "that once within her walls he must assuredly die." For a while he encamped outside of its walls, but being over-persuaded by the doubting philosophers of Anaxagoras, he entered the city, and in a few months he died in a debauch. It is evident that Alexander had much faith in the oracles, as he visited Jupiter Ammon in the Libyan desert, and left many valuable presents.

Plutarch, in writing about the oracles, says: "It would be impossible to enumerate all the instances in which the Pythia proved her power of foretelling events, and the facts of themselves are so well and generally known that it would be useless to bring forth new evidence. Her answers, though submitted to the severest scrutiny, have never proved false or incorrect." And then he cites many instances, among them the eruption of Mount Vesuvius, which overwhelmed the cities of Pompeii and Herculaneum; the defeat of Xerxes' army at Marathon and his navy at Salamis, etc.

Lycurgus, the great Spartan law-giver, consulted the oracle of Delphi. Being satisfied of the correctness of the answer he received, he left his native land never to return.

The most renowned of these oracles were those of Phocis, at Claros in Ionia, at Delos, at Delphi, at Didyma on Mount Ismenus in Bœtia, at Larissa among the Argives, and at Heliopolis in Egypt. The pythonesses or mediums were selected for their great mediumistic power. They were females, virgins of great purity, and they were never allowed to marry. Then, as now, it was a gift confined to the few, and they divined the future and told the past, in many instances, with great accuracy, according to the writings of the ancient historians.

Herodotus and Plutarch give many instances of the truthfulness of these oracles, and relate how the spirits defended the temple at Delphi from the Persians, who went there to pillage it of its vast wealth. "At first the temple was as silent as the grave, then all at once a deafening roar of thunder and flashes of lightning burst forth, and superhuman voices were heard to come forth from the shrine; huge rocks were loosened upon the summit of Parnassus and rolled down amongst the invaders and leveled them like grass. The rest were affrighted and fled in dismay." And this story is as well authenticated as many which are related in the bible of the invisible arm aiding the children of Israel in battle.

Socrates was a clairvoyant medium from his youth. He had unearthly monitions, a "divine voice," as he termed it, attended him; not to urge him to do good, but to restrain from evil. It was equally busy in the most momentous and the most trifling actions of life—at Athens and at Corinth, when he lifted his spear against the enemies of his country; when he bore with meekness the revilings of the shrewish Xantippe; when, in the height of his success, he stood surrounded by Plato, Alcibiades and others of the most noble youths of Greece; and, finally, when he became old and feeble and was persecuted, and he calmly prepared himself to die, this "divine voice" whispered to him sweet words of hope and consolation.

Xenophon said of him, "The little voice" imparted to Socrates a knowledge of the perils that awaited him and of the life to come, which so inspired him that he calmly awaited death as a pleasure that would free him from the mortal body and enable him to assume one of eternal glory.

Plato relates many instances where Socrates gave warnings to his friends of danger, and thereby saved their lives. One he gives of a noble Athenian, Timarchus, "for," said Socrates, "the spirit has just given me the accustomed sign that some danger menaces you." And no one can read of this great philosopher and not be impressed with the idea that he was not in communion with spirits who placed so much wisdom in his mouth.

Gibbon, speaking of Julian, says: "We may learn from his faithful friend, the orator Libanus, that he lived in a perpetual intercourse with the gods and goddesses (the spirits), that they descended upon earth to enjoy the conversation of their favorite hero, that they gently interrupted his slumbers by touching his hands or his hair, that they warned him of every impending danger, and conducted him by their infallible wisdom in every action of his life."

The present forms of communication with the spirits by table-tipping and slate-writing were also well known to the ancients. Ammianus Marcellinus says that in the reign of the Emperor Valens, A. D., 371, some Greeks, skilled in theurgy, were brought to trial for attempting to ascertain, by magic arts, who would succeed to the throne [see page 83]. This mode was similar to that now adopted by many investigators of modern Spiritualism. And Tertullian says, in reproaching some of the Christian fathers: " Do not you, magicians, call ghosts and departed souls from the shades below, and by their infernal charms represent an infinite number of delusions. And how do they perform all this but by the assistance of evil angels and spirits, by which they are able to make stools and tables prophecy." Consequently it is self-evident, whether we take into consideration that evil or good spirits were concerned, that this fact goes to show that seances were held and tables tipped over fifteen centuries ago.

Ancient history is full of instances that go to establish the fact that man had communications with spirits of the departed. The omens that attended the assassination of Cæsar; the apparition of Brutus, at Philippi, and Sylea, the night before he died, saw in a vision the manner of his end. Pliny, the younger, gives an account of a remarkably haunted house that was purchased by the philosopher Athenodorus, on his arrival at Athens. He was struck with its remarkable cheapness, and was informed that no one would live in it. " He said he had nothing to fear." At midnight a noise was heard and the ghastly figure of a skeleton passed through the apartments, dragging a rusty chain, and motioned him to follow. He arose from his table, where he sat writing and followed. The spirit preceded him to an inner court of the mansion and then vanished. He marked the spot by laying some leaves where the apparition designated, and returned to his study. The next morning he sought the magistrates of the city. A search was made and a skeleton loaded with a rusty chain was dug up at the spot that he had marked. He had the skeleton removed and properly interred, and it never appeared again; so it proved a lucky investment.

Macrobius says that Trajan, previous to his invasion of Parthia, consulted the oracle of Heliopolis. It returned a blank sealed paper. At this he laughed and said that as he did not believe in the oracle that they had sent him a proper answer. He sent again, this time the oracle returned a vine cut in pieces and wrapped in a linen cloth, as a symbol that he in like manner should be, should he return. He died in the East and his body was returned, cut up and wrapped in cloth.

Strabo and Pliny assure us that in the reign of Augustus, the priests of a temple at the foot of Mount Loracti, dedicated to the goddess Feronia, had been known to walk barefooted over great quantities of glowing embers; and Strabo says, " The same ordeal was practiced by the priestesses of the goddess Astabores in Cappadocia."

In speaking of mediums among the ancients, a writer in the *London Examiner* says:

" How many persons who practice, or who discredit the fashionable exercise of table-turning and spirit-invoking are aware that, ages ago, before our ancestors had tables to turn, the process was a well recognized one in Imperial Rome and Constantinople? Of abnormal manifestations of disturbance in the ordinary range of nobility among human beings, we hear nothing in ancient history, but we hear enough of the manner in which the Greeks and Romans in early Christian ages endeavored by assumed spiritual agency, to influence the movements of the legs of tables, to make us sensible that modern processes for effecting the same end, are inferior in point of elegance and awe-inspiring effect. This, we think, will scarcely be denied by those best acquainted with the present method of conducting a seance when they learn the Roman method of operation, which was as follows: When a family or an individual desired to obtain information in regard to some friend beyond the pale of human knowledge, recourse was had to a priest, that is, a professor practiced in the arts of superhuman intelligence. Accordingly, when the appointed day came, the officiating medium appeared in white, and bearing in his hands a small table standing on a tripod base. Pausing at the entrance door he waited till the threshold and the atrium had been sprinkled with aromatic and symbolic fluids before he passed on into the principal apartment of the house, and deposited his tripod over the center of the floor. This table, which, as we are informed, must be made of laurel-wood, cut under awe-inspiring auspices, had attached to its base a metallic hoop encircling it, on which the letters of the Greek alphabet were graven, while its upper rim bore a number of catgut strings, to which a silvered leaden ball was suspended. When, after due course of prayers, incantations and various gentle aids to motion, the table began to rotate, the priest and his attendants, who sat on the floor, forming a circle round it, noted down each letter that was in turn touched by the extending strings of the rotating tripod. These letters were put together, and the words they formed accepted as the answer of the oracle. In the case of table-turning in the latter days of the Empire, which has been trasmitted to us, we find that a body of conspirators, being desirous of ascertaining if the pretender Theodorus, whose cause they advocated, would be the successor of the Emperor Valens, tested the question by this interdicted mode of divination; and conceiving that the letters *Th E O D* had been struck, there could be no doubt of the fulfillment of their wishes, they hastily overthrew the table, hurried the priests out of the house, and dispersed, lest their evil deeds might be detected by the Imperial officers appointed to enforce the penalties incurred by dealers in magic. Fate, however, was too strong for them, for Theodorus was seized and put to death, as history can testify, while Theodosius succeeded to Valens, and thus relieved the oracle from the charge of mendacity."

But we need not marvel at these strange stories of profane history, for the Holy Bible is filled with it, from Genesis to Revelations. Aaron's rod was turned into a serpent and swallowed up the rods transformed into serpents by the Egyptian magicians. The Hebrew children walked through the fiery furnace; Jacob wrestled with an angel; the walls of Jericho were overthrown at the sound of a ram's horn; Lot's wife was turned into a pillar of salt; the witch of Endor raised the spirit of Samuel; Abraham conversed with angels and ate veal cutlets with them in his tent; and a voice cried out to Abraham and told him of a ram entangled in the vines, which he could offer on his altar as a sacrifice, instead of his son Isaac; Elijah was fed by the ravens; the children of Israel were fed with manna; Christ on the mount of Transfiguration saw and talked with Moses and Elias; Peter was let out of prison; and Christ rose from the dead.

CHAPTER IX.

Christianity

Christianity comes from the Greek word Christos which signifies ~~unction~~ over or *anointed*, and is the same as the translation of the Hebrew word *Messiah*, *Messias*, or *Mashiach*. These words alike mean the *anointed one* Kings and high-priests were consecrated to their office by being anointed. The *anointed one*, therefore, means the chosen, ordained, crowned or consecrated to a high office; *christuomai* signifies to be good, kind and merciful; *christotheia* signifies goodness of heart, *chresteriso* signifies to prophesy, *chrestes* means a prophet, *chresmos* is the oracle or the divine response and *chrisma* is the anointing oil which was anciently freely used on Christian converts and still continues in the unction of the Catholic church. Thus *chres* or *chris* is the Greek expression for that which is good and beautiful, or which comes from heaven The word christos was so closely associated with divinity that it was often applied by the Greeks to Apollo and other gods The world has had many christos or saviors, and all nations have had their christos or christs. Therefore Jesus Christ is the name applied to the Hebrew christos, the anointed prophet. Mary used oil to anoint Christ, and wiped his feet with her hair to show her profound veneration for him.

Christianity is a name full of power and eloquent meaning, a divine and inspired religion, full of love and heroism It cannot be monopolized by the believers in Jesus Christ, but includes all who embrace and follow the instructions of Jesus Christ and imitate his purity of life, and who attempt to live in perfect accord with the divine law, so as to embody in themselves the highest inspiration of which he is capable.

It allows a large range of belief and worship. One may be a Christian and believe that Christ was only a good man, another may believe Christ a god equal to the father in heaven, and he can be a Christian, another can worship the Virgin Mary, his mother, and be a Christian Anyone may be a Christian if he goes to church and contributes to the support of the gospel, in a word all who belong to the Christian nations, whether he be a Jew or Gentile, Atheist or Infidel, is according to the definition of the term, a Christian It represents and expresses a civilization.

Advent of Christ.

The time was propitious for the introduction of a new religion Paganism was in its last throes; Jupiter's, Manu's and Moses' altars had no longer believers, and the intelligent people had discarded the myth, and the masses were ready to swallow any new religion offered Pythagoras, Aristotle, Socrates, Plato and Cicero had evicted the myth of the Olympian gods from the minds of the intelligent thinking people. Their writings, like that of modern science, had undermined the dogmas of the fabulous mythology Cicero wondered that two priests could look into each other's faces and not laugh at the trick. For two ages past, Pyrrha, Cimon, Sextus, Empiricus and Enesidius no longer believed in anything and Lucretius had just written his book on nature.

On the other side, those old and decaying theologies of Moses left in the spirit of the multitude the idea of a Redeemer, which ancient India had bequeathed to all the nations; and the wearied people waited for something new to replace their extinct beliefs, to nourish their energy, paralyzed by doubt, and in great need of hope.

It was then that a poor Jew, born of the lower class, appeared, possessed of remarkable mediumistic power, and started on the mission of reforming man and checking the growth of materialism He soon gathered around him many followers, and persecution did its work "and the blood of martyrs became the seed of the church."

Primitive Christianity had its origin in small scattered groups, organized into secret societies with passwords, grips and signs, which enabled the initiated to recognize each other. To avoid the unrelenting persecutions of their enemies they were obliged to meet in the night in secret places; in caves, deserted catacombs, woods and mountain fastnesses From the first appearance of Jesus and his twelve disciples, they sought refuge in quiet places, in the wilderness and among their friends in Bethany It is evident that they were rather quiet and did not attract much attention among the profane writers. Renan shows that Philo, who lived in Palestine while the "glad tidings" were being preached, never heard of him. Josephus, the Hebrew historian, who was born three years after the crucifixion of Christ, only makes a short mention of him, and even that bears the marks of interpolation

Suetonius, the secretary of Adrian, who wrote the history of the Emperor Claudius in the second century, says that he (Claudius) banished all the Jews, who were continually making disturbances at the instigation of one *Crestus*, evidently meaning Christ

The Emperor Adrian, in a letter to Servianus, says, "That he believes the new sect (Christians) were worshipers of Serapis, an Egyptian deity; and Christ is represented as Serapis, wearing long hair, turned back, falling down on his back and shoulders like a woman, his whole person enveloped in drapery, reaching his feet." [See "Gnostics and their Remains," page 68] "There can be no doubt," remarks the same author, "that the head of Serapis, marked, as the face is, by a grave and pensive majesty, supplied the first idea for the conventional portraits of the Savior."

The Gnosis, or Gnosticism, comprehended the doctrine of the magi—the wise men of the East who followed the star to Bethlehem—and they were in direct communication with the Divine mind, which revealed to them these facts, through some of the modes of spiritual manifestation. They were not Jews, they were heathen who had come from the East, and were skilled in the arts of nature and knew by certain signs they were to know him, and so informed Herod of his whereabouts.

Christ said, "God is a spirit and they who worship him worship in spirit and truth " Those who follow Christ's teachings embrace the doctrines of Spiritualism, and consequently there should be no antagonism between Spiritualism and the other Christian religions, as they are all derived from the same source. Christ said, "I will be with you even to the end of the world " He evidently meant that his spirit would be with them And the idea that Christ would come again and reign on earth was taken from the mistaken idea that he should be reincarnated in the flesh again, which is the belief of the Buddhists that Buddha is ever reincarnating in the person of a child.

Christ and his apostles were possessed of wonderful mediumistic powers, but in time this mediumistic power was lost in the cold embrace of the Christian churches, who did not follow his sublime teachings and preach his gospel to the whole world. In losing this mediumistic power the churches have become materialistic, and for that reason they oppose the doctrine of modern Spiritualism, which is intended to take man back to the pure stream of religion that he taught in his sermon on the mount. Christ received his messages direct from the Divine mind, and there is no reason why it cannot be done by others as well as by him.

The laws of the natural and spirit world are always the same Philo and other contemporary historians say the Essenes were a sect of pure and holy men, which arose about one hundred years before the advent of Jesus of Nazareth; and it is supposed by some that he belonged to that order. The doctrines, manners and customs of this sect resembled that of Jesus and his disciples, and his sermon on the mount is full of their aphorisms This pure and simple spiritual religion taught by the early Christians perished about the time that Constantine the Great usurped its name and fame in order to justify his own iniquitous and atrocious murders, and to give him strength by enlisting the Christians under his banner; and it then became engrafted on Roman paganism. The shaved headed augurs were changed into monks and priests, and the vestal virgins into nuns and sisters of charity; and the burning of incense, is a vestige of the fire-worshipers, who always kept a fire burning in a lamp suspended near or on the altar. After it became the state religion, with the Emperor Constantine at its head, it assumed a power that enforced its creeds upon the unbelievers, that made the name of Jesus known to the whole Roman empire, which at that time governed the civilized world.

Ammonius Sacchas, the great Alexandrian teacher and philosopher, the *throdiaoktis*, in his numerous works a century and a half before St. Augustine, acknowledged Jesus as "an excellent man, and the friend of God." He always maintained that the ultimate design of Jesus was not to abolish the intercourse with gods and demons (spirits), but simply to purify the ancient religion; that "the religion of the multitude went hand in hand with philosophy, and with her had shared the fate of being by degrees corrupted and obscured with mere human conceits, superstitions and lies, that it ought, therefore, to be brought back to its *original purity*, by purging it of this dross and expounding it upon philosophical principles; and that all Christ had in view was to reinstate and restore to its primitive integrity and purity the wisdom of the ancients."

All great religious reformers were pure at the beginning. The first followers of Buddha as well as the disciples of Jesus were men of great austerity and the highest morality, as in the case of Sakya-Muni, Pythagoras, Plato, Jesus, St. Paul, Ammonius and Sakkas. The great Gnostic leaders, if less successful, were not less virtuous in practice nor less morally pure. Marcion, Basilides and Valentinus were renowned for their ascetic lives. The Nicolaitanes, if they did not belong to the great body of the Ophites, were numbered among the small sects which were absorbed in it at the beginning of the second century. The Gnostics were a sect of philosophers that arose in the first century of Christianity, and they formed a system of theology agreeable to that of Pythagoras and

Plato, and in conformity to that of the scriptures They held that all religions had their origin in secret societies

The innumerable gems and amulets are a proof of this. They had their symbols, signs and secret workings that the outside world knew nothing of, by which means they were able to know each other. The Kabalists were the first to embellish the universal Logos with such terms as "Light of Light," the messenger of *life and light* (see John 1), and we find these expressions adopted *in toto* by the Christians, with the addition of nearly all the Gnostic terms, such as Pleroma (fullness), Archons, Æons, etc, as to the "*first born*," the first and the "only begotten" These terms are as old as the world Origen shows the word "Logos," as existing among the Brahmins. The Brahmins say that the God is *light*, not such as one sees, nor such as sun and fire; but they have the *God Logos*, not articulate, the Logos of the Gnosis, through whom the highest mysteries of the Gnosis are seen by the wise—those of clairvoyant sight The Acts and the fourth Gospel are full of Gnostic expressions. The Kabalistic terms "God's first-born emanated from the Most High," together with that *which is the* "*spirit of the anointed;*" and again, "they called Him the anointed of the highest," are reproduced in spirit and substance by the author of the *Gospel of St. John.* "That was the *true light*, and the light shineth in darkness" "And the word was *made flesh.*"

The "Christ" and the "Logos" are terms which existed ages before Christianity. The Oriental Gnosis was studied long before the days of Moses, and we have to seek for the origin of all these words in the Archaic periods of the primeval Asiatic philosophy. Peter's second epistle and Jude's fragment, preserved in the new Testament, show by their phraseology that they belonged to the Kabalistic Oriental order, for they use the same expressions as did the Christian Gnostics, who built or took a part of their system from the Oriental Kabala, and that it was grafted on it. "Presumptuous are they [the Ophites], self-willed, they are not afraid to speak evil of dignities," says Peter in Second Epistle, ii. 10 The original model for the latter is the abusive Tertullian and Irenæus. "Likewise (even as Sodom and Gomorrah) also, these filthy dreamers defile the flesh, despise *dominion* and speak evil of *dignities*," says Jude, repeating the very words of Peter and thereby using expressions consecrated in the Kabala. *Dominion* is the "empire," the *tenth* of the Kabalistic sephiron. They held that the types of the creation, or the attributes of the Supreme Being, are through the emanations of Adam Kadmon.

Thus, when the Nazarenes and other Gnostics of the more Platonic tendency twitted the Jews as "abortions who worship their god Qurbo, *Adonai*," we need not wonder at the wrath of those who had accepted the old Mosaic system, but at that of Peter and Jude, who claimed to be followers of Jesus, and dissent from the views of him who also was a Nazarene. The dispersed Nazarenes were a secret sect that had no affiliation with the Jews, and they were a remnant of the ancient Phœnicians, that still lived on the other side of the Jordan and extended far into the interior.

According to the Kabala, the *empire* of *dominion* is "the consuming fire and his wife is the temple or church, and powers and dignities (spirits) are subordinate genii of the archangels and angels of the Sohar." These emanations are the very life and soul of the Kabala and Zoroasterism. And the Talmud, the sacred book of the Jews, is borrowed from the Zend-Avesta, the sacred book or bible of the Persians and fire-worshipers; therefore, by adopting the views of Peter, Jude and other apostles, the Christians have become but a dissenting sect of the Persians, for they do not even interpret the meaning of all such *powers* as the true Kabalists do.

St. Paul, warning his converts against the worshiping of angels, showed how well he appreciated, even so early as his period, the dangers of borrowing from a mythical doctrine, the philosophy of which could be rightly interpreted but by its well-learned adherents, the Magi and the Jewish Tanaim. In Colossians ii: 18, he says, "Let no man beguile you of your reward in a voluntary humanity and worshiping of angels, intruding into those things which he hath not seen, vainly puffed up by his fleshly mind," is a sentence laid right at the door of Peter and his companions.

In the Talmud Michael is prince of water, who has *seven* inferior spirits subordinate to him. He is the patron, the guardian angel of the Jews, as Daniel informs us. And the Greek Ophites, who identified him with their Ophimorphous, the personified creation of envy and malice, of Ilda-Baoth, thet Demiurgus (creator of the material world), and undertook to prove that he, Samuel, the Hebrew prince of the evil spirits or Persian deos, were naturally regarded by the Jews as blasphemers.

In all ages and among all nations there is a tendency of the ignorant and designing to create gods out of ministering spirits and angels that come in contact with mediums, seers and prophets, which soon corrupts the pure and monotheistic belief in one God, out of whose divine will and power all things have evolved.

It is evident that Jesus was a pure and good man, endowed with a great love of the pure and simple religion, and it is clearly apparent that he struggled hard to reform the Jews; but they did not understand and appreciate him, and they therefore crucified him; and after the elapse of three hundred years he was deified as one of the godhead, and from his teachings and those of his disciples, has arisen the Christian church, and over the question of his divinity rivers of blood have been shed to make him a god, and to enforce the creeds and dogmas of the church.

St. Paul was the true founder of Christian theology. This indomitable disciple was a man of learning, well versed in the mysterious doctrines of the Gnostics, and wrote in the true Kabalistic spirit of the masters of the Lord Jesus Christ; and the manner of his conversion is one of the best physical manifestations of the spirits on record. It is evident that St. Paul, believing in occult powers in the world, "unseen," but ever "present," says, "Ye walked according to the *æon* of this world, according to Archon (*Ilda Baoth*, the *Demiurg*), that has the *domination* of the *air*," and "we wrestle not against flesh and blood, but against the *dominations*, the *powers*, the lords of darkness, the mischievousness of spirits in the upper regions." This sentence "ye were dead in sin and error," for "ye walked according to the Archon," or (Ilda-Baoth,) the god and creator and master of the Ophites, shows unequivocally that, 1st, Paul, notwithstanding some dissensions with the more important doctrines of the Gnostics, shared more or less their cosmogonical views on the emanations; 2d, that he was fully aware that this Demiurg, whose Jewish name was Jehovah, was not the God preached by Jesus; and now, if we compare the doctrine of St. Paul with the religious views of Peter and Jude, we find that not only did they worship Michael, the archangel, but that they also *reverenced Satan*, because the latter was also an angel before his fall. This they do quite openly, and abuse the Gnostics for speaking "evil" of him. (See Peter's Second Epistle).

No one can deny the following: Peter, when denouncing those who are not afraid to speak evil of "*dignities*," adds immediately, "whereas angels which are greater in power and might bring not railing accusations against them (the dignities) before the Lord." Who are the "dignities" referred to? Jude, in his general epistle, makes the meaning of the word as clear as day. The "dignities" are the devils, and the devils are evil spirits. Jude when complaining of the disrespect shown by the Gnostics to *powers and dominions*, uses the very words of Peter: "And yet Michael, the archangel, when contending with the devil (evil spirit) he disputed about the body of Moses, *durst not bring against him a railing accusation*, but said, 'the Lord rebuke thee.'" Is this not plain enough to show that they did? if not then we have the Kabala to prove who were the dignities.

In Deuteronomy xxxiv: 6, we find that the "Lord Himself buried Moses in a valley of Moab, and no man knoweth of his sepulchre unto this day." This biblical *lapsus linguæ* of Jude gives a strong coloring to the assertions of some of the Gnostics. They claimed only what was secretly taught by the Jewish Kabalists themselves, to-wit: that the highest supreme God was unknown and invisible, "the king of light is a closed eye;" that Ilda-Baoth, the Jewish second Adam, was the real Demiurg; and that Iao, Adonai, Sáboth and Eloi were the quaternary emanations which formed the unity of the God of the Hebrews—Jehovah. Moreover, the latter was also called Michael, the archangel, by Samuel, and re-

garded as an angel several degrees removed from the godhead. The disciples were uneducated, except St. Paul, and they drew their knowledge from the unseen world like many of the mediums of modern Spiritualism, who often confound the most learned doctors and men of science.

The Chaldean version of the Pentateuch, made by the well-known Babylonian divine Onkelos, was regarded as the most authoritive of all; and it is according to this learned rabbi that Hillel, and and other tanaim after him, held that the being who appeared to Moses in the burning bush, on Mount Sinai, and who finally buried him, was the angel of the Lord, Memro, and not the Lord himself, and that he whom the Hebrews of the old Testament mistook for Iahoh, was his messenger, one of his sons or emanations. All this goes to establish but one logical conclusion, merely that the Gnostics were far superior to the disciples in knowledge, learning and the religious doctrines of the Jews.

There have existed in all ages men who belonged to secret societies under different names —Esoteric, Brahminical, Buddhistical, Chaldean, Hermetic, Ophite, Gymnosophites and Magi philosophers. The Sufis and Rashees, of Kashmere, instituted a kind of international and universal Freemasonry among the Esoteric societies; and says Higgins, "These Rashees are the Essenians, Carmelites or Nazarites of the Temple, and it was from the latter Christ derived his knowledge, as he was a Nazarene, and the priest or masters understood the occult science, under the name of Regenerating Fire." This science for more than three thousand years was the peculiar possession of the Indian and Egyptian priesthood, into the knowledge of which Moses was initiated at Heliopolis, where he was educated; and Jesus was educated among the Essenian priests of Egypt or Judea, and by the knowledge thus gained these two great reformers, particularly the latter, wrought many of the miracles mentioned in the scriptures."

"The Christian Gnostics sprang into existence towards the beginning of the second century, and just at the time when the Essenes most mysteriously faded away, which indicates that they were the identical Essenes, and, moreover, pure *Christists,* viz: they believed, and were those who best understood what one of their own brethren had preached. In insisting that the letter Iota, mentioned by Jesus, (Mat. v.18,) indicated a secret doctrine in relation to the ten æons, is sufficient to demonstrate to a Kabalist that Jesus belonged to the Free-masonry of those days; for I, which is iota in Greek, has no other name in other languages, and is, as it was among the Gnostics of those days, a pass-word, meaning the ' Scripture of the Father,' in Eastern brotherhoods which exist to this day."

"It comes to this," writes Irenæus, complaining of the Gnostics, "they neither consent to the scriptures nor tradition;" and why should we wonder at that, when even the commentators of the nineteenth century, with nothing but fragments of Gnostic manuscripts to compare with the voluminous writings of their calumniators, have been enabled to detect fraud on every page? How much more must the polished and learned Gnostics, with all their advantages of personal observation and knowledge of the facts, have realized the stupendous scheme of fraud that was being consummated before their very eyes? Why should they accuse Celsus of maintaining that their religion was all based on the speculations of Plato, with the difference that his doctrines were far more pure and rational than theirs, when we find Sprengell, seventeen centuries later, writing the following· "Not only did they (the Christians) think to discover the dogmas of Plato in the books of Moses, but, moreover, they fancied that by introducing Platonism into Christianity they would *elevate* the *dignity* of this religion and make it more popular among the nations."

"They introduced it so well that not only was the Platonic philosophy selected as a basis for the trinity, but even the legends and mythical stories which had been current among the admirers of the great philosopher, as a time-honored custom required in the eyes of his posterity such an allegorical homage to every hero worthy of deification, were revamp-ed and used by the Christians. Without going so far as India, did they not have a ready model for the 'miraculous conception' in the legend about Periktione, Plato's mother? In her case it was also maintained by popular tradition that she had immaculately conceived him, and that the god Apollo was his father Even the annunciation by an angel to Joseph, in a dream, the Christians copied from the message of Apollo to Aristow, Periktione's husband, that the child to be born from her was the offspring of that god So, too, Romulus, one of the founders of Rome, was said to be the son of Mars by the virgin Rhea Sylvia, and he was suckled and nurtured by a wolf and was afterwards deified "

The birth and the wonderful manifestations that are related of Christ, was one of the legends peculiar to that age. To enshroud it in mystery and to make it miraculous was to give to him the prestige of a god, when in reality he only claimed to be the son of man, and when we make due allowance for it we are left to wonder how it was ever possible that any one should look upon him otherwise than as a good man, who was conceived, born, lived and died as other men How he could be held as other than a man surpasses my comprehension, and how the intelligent, thinking people of the nineteenth century can think he was a god is evidence of credulity, stupidity and ignorance

It is evident that the Gnostics had a better and more correct knowledge of the teachings of Christ and his disciples than those who claim to be founders of the modern Christianity, which did not have its rise until in the third century, and we should be willing to give to them the credit of being as honest as any other sect. And if we can believe Nicholas of Antioch, a man of honest repute, full of the holy ghost and wisdom, we must come to the conclusion that Christ was simply a good man with lofty thoughts, a great love of humanity, and clear perception of right, added to his great mediumistic powers.

CHAPTER X.

ALL RELIGIONS APPEAR TO HAVE ONE COMMON ORIGIN   THE ORIGIN OF THE
TRINITY, CROSS, SACRED RIVERS, MADONNA, ARK, DELUGE, FISH STORY.

The Olympus of the Greeks is but a reproduction of the Hindoo Olympus. The legend of Jason and the Golden Fleece is still in the mouth of every one in India, and the Iliad of Homer is nothing but an echo and enfabled souvenir of the Ramayana, a Hindoo poem, in which Rama goes at the head of his allies to recover his wife, Sita, who had been carried off by the King of Ceylon; while the Greeks immortalized it in Homer, where Paris carried off the fair Helen to Troy.

Æsop and Babrias copied Hindoo fables that reached them through Russia, Syria and Egypt. Babrias, though a Greek, says at the commencement of his second proem that it came from the East; and Jacolliot says that no one can read the fables of the Hindoo Pilpay, or the Brahmin Ramdamyayer, without being impressed with the idea that they are the original, and that Æsop, Babrias and La Fontaine are plagiarists, and that the Greek and modern fabulists have not taken the trouble to change the action of these little dramas.

One nation copies from another like individuals, and the succeeding generations retain the history and traditions of their ancestors. The Greek language and religion has been taken from the Hindoo. As the Sanscrit is the mother of the Greek language, so the Brahmin religion and laws are more or less copied into the Greek and Roman religion and laws   Homer and Virgil, Sophocles and Euripides, Plautus and Terence, copied, altered and modified the poetry of the Brahmins, while Socrates, Pythagoras, Plato and Aristotle have drawn their inspiration from an older and a more ancient philosophy of the Brahmins, Egyptians and Persians. Titus, Livius, Sallust, Herodotus and Tacitus are our models as historians, and they only copied from others still older, dating farther back in time. The Justinian code has been taken from the Hindoo code of Manu, as it bears the ear-marks of legislation, marriage, filiation, parental authority, tutelage, adoption, property, the laws of contract, deposit, loan, sale, partnership, donations and testaments.

Manu, Manes, Minos and Moses were all great law-givers and legislators. These four names overshadow the entire ancient world. They appear at the beginning of the four different nations, and they play the same role, surrounded by the same mysterious halo. All of the four were legislators and high-priests, and all four founded theocratic and sacerdotal societies   That they stand in relation to each other as predecessor and successor, however distant, seems proven by the similitude of name and identity of the institutions they created. " In Sanscrit *Manu* signifies *the man par excellence*, the legislator. Manes, Minos and Moses, do they not betray an incontestible unity of derivation from the Sanscrit with the slight variations of different periods, and the different languages in which they are written, Egyptian, Greek and Hebrew?"

Manu, the philosopher and law-giver of India, and Manes, the Egyptian legislator, are extensively copied   A Cretan visits Egypt to study her institutions, which he introduces into his own country, and history preserves his memory under the name of Minos. Moses is the liberator of the servile caste of Hebrews from out of bondage in Egypt. These laws are all claimed to have been given to them by God, out of which they have created caste, which in India has crushed the masses down in ignorance and superstition, and it made all subservient to the Brahmins, who really were the governing class. Moses created the order of Levi, the priests who claimed that God governed them, but they ate the offerings, collected the tithes and ruled the people. The Roman people were divided up into castes—priests, senators, patricians and plebeians—which was a feebler imitation of the Hindoo society. Such has ever been the Jaws and religions, "*Divide, corrumpe et impera!*" divide, demoralize and govern.

The Vedic civilization, under the Hindoo priests (the Brahmins), like that of Egypt under der Manes, crushed the masses into a nation of slaves, which deprived them of all social and political rights, making them mere machines to produce, that the privileged classes may live in luxury and splendor. The Roman hierarchy for ages has kept the masses in ignorance, that they might govern them, and at one time their power was so great that they even scourged kings and forced them to do penance.

"Excommunication was nothing else than a weapon of despotism, picked up in the pagodas of Brahma, for the subjugation of people and for the triumph of the priests. We have seen Savonarola die at the stake for having exposed the disorders of Alexander VI; and the pious Robert of France, abandoned by his friends and his faithful servants, obliged to bend the knee under the hand of a religious fanatic Human hecatombs have been burning on the piles of faith and the altar reddened with blood. Ages have passed away; we are but wakening to progress and freethought. But let us expect struggles without end until the day shall come when we shall have courage to arraign all sacerdotalism at the bar of liberty."

The Hindoos, in their primitive times, had their virgins attached to the service of the pagodas, some tended the sacred fire, which burned day and night before the holy trinity, and never was allowed to go out; others, on days of procession, danced before the car or ark as it was carried through the villages, others, under the delirium produced by an exciting beverage which is known to the Brahmins, uttered oracles in the sanctuaries to fakirs and sunniassys (holy mendicants), or to extort from

the amazed people, abundant offering of fruit rice, cattle and money; others sung sacred hymns at the sacrifices and festivals and at funerals, religion requiring each son to make offerings on the recurring anniversary of his father's and mother's deaths, and, as no man could be admitted into heaven who had not a son to make this offering, so this accounts for the great desire of men of the Aryan race to have a son to inherit his name The consecrated virgins of Egypt danced before the statues of the gods, the pythonesses of Delphi, the priestesses of Ceres, who delivered oracles, the vestal virgins of Rome who tended the sacred fire, and the sisters of charity, were but heirs to the devadassa of India This tradition of the woman, virgin and priestess is so much of an oriental inspiration that we see all the nations of antiquity reject it as they gradually emancipated themselves from superstition and mystery. If, then, it appears but a legacy from the primitive cradle, nothing is more natural than to trace it to the country whence departed the colonizing tribes

Jesus is a Sancrit word signifying pure essence, which is the root, the radical origin of a large number of ancient names used alike for gods and distinguished men, such as Isis, the mother of Horus, the female principle in nature, the Earth, the Egyptian goddess; Josue, in Hebrew; Joshua the successor of Moses; Josias, king of the Hebrews; and Jeseus or Jesus, in Hebrew Jeosuah, which name is very common with the Hebrews, was in ancient India the tiller, the consecrated epithet assigned to all incarnations "The officiating Bohemians in temples and pagodas now accord this title of Jeseus, or pure essence, or divine emanation, only to Chrisna, who is alone recognized as the word, the true incarnation by the Vishnuites and freethinkers of Brahminism." (See "India Bible," by Jacolliot, page 108.) Hence comes the word Jesus Christ, from Jezeus—Chrisna—of the Sancrit.

Chrisna, Buddha, Zoroaster, Christ and Mohammed have all played a human role, and God has judged them as he has all the rest of mankind, according to the good they have accomplished These great and good men started out for a high and noble purpose, but their successors, more cunning than their masters, having made them gods to smooth their own way, present themselves to the people as celestial messengers, and thus sanctify their ambitious purposes, and rule and govern man. On a careful and critical examination they all teach the same thing; all tell about the same story. It is the same, revamped to suit the age and the nation in which they lived.

The Egyptian god Bacchus was brought up at Mysa, and is famous as having been the conqueror of India. In Egypt he was called Osiris; in India Dionysius, and not improbably Krishna or Chrisna, which means a savior, as he was called Adoneus, which signifies the Lord of heaven, or the Lord and giver of light in Arabia, and liber throughout the Roman dominions, from whence is derived our term liberal for everything that is generous, frank and amiable. He manifested his glory in the wine, therefore he is sometimes called the god of wine. It is evident that he was one of the sun-gods of some of the ancients, as we find expressions like these used in his worship: Io Terombe, *let us cry unto the Lord;* Io or Ia Baccoth, *God sees our tears;* Jehovah Evan! Hevoe! and Eloah, *the author of our existence, the mighty God;* Hu Esh, *thou art the fire;* Elta Esh, *thou art the life;* and Io Nissi, *O Lord, direct us;* which last is the literal English of the Latin motto in the arms of the city of London, retained to this day, "*Domine dirige nos.*" The Romans, out of all these terms, preferred the name of Baccoth, out of which they composed Bacchus. The more delicate ear of the Greeks was better pleased with the words Io Nissi, out of which they formed Dionysius.

The three letters I H S, surrounded with rays of glory, that are so often seen hanging in the Catholic churches and burying grounds, which are supposed to stand for *Jesus Homineum Salvator,* is none other than the identical name of Bacchus, *Yes,* exhibited in Greek letters, *V H E,* (see Hesychius on the word *V H E, i. e., Y e s,* Bacchus, Sol, the Sun). And the feast of Bacchus was always celebrated by drinking wine and eating bread, from which the Christians derived the idea of the sacrament. One of the odes of Anacreon, translated, reads thus: "To arms! But I shall

drink; boy, bring me the goblet, for I would rather lie dead drunk than dead."

In the ancient Orphic verses, sung in the orgies of Bacchus, as celebrated throughout Egypt, Phœnicia, Syria, Arabia, Asia Minor, Greece, and ultimately in Italy, it is related how that god, who had been born in Arabia, was picked up in a box that floated on the water, and took his name *Mises,* in signification of his having been saved from the water, and Bimater from his having had two mothers; that is, one by nature and another who had adopted him. He had a rod with which he performed miracles, and which he could change into a serpent at pleasure. He passed the Red Sea dry-shod at the head of his army; he divided the waters of the rivers Orontes and Hydraspus by the touch of his rod and passed through them dry-shod. By the same mighty rod he drew water from the rock, and wherever he marched the land flowed with milk and honey. And the similarity of these verses shows that Moses copied them or that they were taken from him.

The Egyptian tau or cross (T) was in use many centuries earlier than the period assigned to Abraham, the alleged forefather of the Israelites, for Moses directed the children of Israel to mark their door-posts and lintels with blood, lest the "Lord God" might make a mistake and kill them instead of the Egyptians, and this mark is a tau, the identical Egyptian handle-cross, with the half of which talisman Horus raised the dead, as is shown on a sculptured ruin at Philæ. And it is asserted that the rod of Moses, which he used to perform his miracles before Pharaoh, was no doubt a *crux ansata,* or something like it, as used by the Egyptian priests. In the ancient Hebrew the sign of the cross was formed thus X, but in the original Egyptian hieroglyphics it is the same as a perfect Christian cross †.

According to King and other numismatists and archæologists, the cross was a symbol of eternal life. A tau or Egyptian cross was used in the mysteries of Bacchus and Eleusinia. It was laid on the breast of the initiate, as a symbol of the "new birth;" that his spiritual birth had regenerated and united his astral soul with his divine spirit, and that he was ready to ascend in spirit to the blessed abodes of light and g ory. The tau is a magic talisman and at the same time is a religious emblem. It was adopted by the Christians, through the Gnostics and Kabalists, who used it largely, as their numerous gems testify. They took the tau, or handle-cross, from the Egyptians, and the Latin cross from the Buddhist museums, who brought it from India, where it can be found to have been in use for two or three centuries before Christ. The cross was known to the ancient Assyrians, Egyptians, Armenians, Hindoos and Romans, long before the crucifixion of Christ

The Brah-matma, the chief of the Hindoo initiates, had on his head-gear two keys, which were symbols of the revealed mystery of life and death, and were placed cross-wise, and in some of the Buddhist pagodas of Tartary and Mongolia, the entrance to a chamber within the temple is generally ornamented with a cross, formed of two fishes, and so are the zodiacs of the ancient Chaldeans and Buddhists represented with crossed fishes And even Solomon's temple was built on these foundations, forming the "triple tau" or three crosses, according to one of the traditions of ancient Masonry.

In its mystical sense the Egyptian cross derives its origin from its former use as an emblem of the realization by the earliest philosophers of an androgynous dualism in every manifestation of nature, which proceeds from the abstract idea of a likewise androgynous or double-sexed (male and female) deity. The tau or Egyptian cross, in its mystical sense as well as the *crux ansata*, represents the "*tree of life*," while the Roman cross, on which Christ was crucified, was called the "*tree of infamy*." The crucifix was an instrument of torture, and was common among the Romans, for it was unknown among Semitic nations until conquered by the Romans, and during the first two decades after the crucifixion of Christ, the apostles looked upon it with horror It is certainly not the Christian cross that John had in mind, when speaking of the signet of the "living God," but the mystic tau.

Many customs found in Christendom may be traced back to Egypt. The Egyptian at his marriage put a gold ring on his wife's finger as a token that he entrusted her with all his

property, just as in a Church of England marriage service the bridegroom does the same thing, saying, "with all my worldly goods I thee endow." The feast of candles at Isis is still marked in the Christian calendar as Candlemas-day. The Catholic priests shave their heads as the ancient Egyptian priests did several thousand years ago The surplice of the Episcopal minister, which he wears when reading the liturgy is the same as that worn by the ancient Egyptian priest. The Pope assuming to hold the keys, was taken from an Egyptian priest at Thebes whose "title was keeper of the two doors of heaven," (see Sharpe's "Egyptian Mythology ") All the forms and ceremonies of the Jews bear ear-marks of having been borrowed by Moses from the Egyptians, "the ark," "the holy of holies," the scapegoat, the cherubim, were derived from the sphynx. Also the rite of circumcision was practiced in Egypt as early as the fourth dynasty, says Wilkinson, long before the time of Abraham.

The Trinity

In the Book of Hermes, the origin of which is lost in the colonization of Egypt, there is a reference made to the Hindoo Chrisna, according to the Brahmins, and it enunciates in distinct terms the trinitarian dogma. "The light is me," says Pimander; "*the Divine thought; I am the nous*, or intelligence, and I am thy God and am far older than the human principle, which escapes from the shadow. I am the germ of thought, the resplendent word; the Son of God. Think that what thou seest and hearest is the *verbum* of the master; it is the thought which is God, the Father. The celestial ocean, the ETHER, which flows from east to west, is the breath of the Father, the life-giving principle, the Holy Ghost, for they are not separated and their union is LIFE."

The trinity of the Egyptians was a triangle Plutarch says that the Egyptians worshiped Osiris, Isis and Horus, under the form of a triangle. He adds that they considered everything perfect to have three parts, and therefore their good god made himself three-fold, while their god of evil remained single

The ancient Hindoos had a Christ, a virgin "mother of God," queen of heaven, though Isis is also by right the queen of heaven, and is generally represented carrying in her hand the *crux ansata* (☥) or cross. In one of the ancient tombs of the Pharaohs there is a figure of the birth of the sun in the form of a little child issuing from the bosom of its divine mother, the resplendent golden rays darting forth from its head, which was intended to represent the rays of the sun-god. The monogram or symbol of the god Saturn was the sign of the cross with a ram's horn in indication of the lamb of God. Jupiter also bore a cross with a horn, and Venus a cross with a circle.

Among the Semitic nations we can trace the trinity to the prehistoric days of the fabled Sesostris, who is identified by more than one critic with Nimrod the "mighty hunter." "Tell me, O, thou strong in fire, who, before me, could subjugate all things? and who shall after me?" And the oracle saith thus: "First, God, then the Word and then the Spirit." (See "Ap Malal," liber I, cap. iv.)

Then there was the trinity of God, earth, atmosphere; earth, fire and water; and this threefold function of the Divinity evidently gave rise to the Hebrew Jehovah, or Ye-ho-vah, representing the Future, the Present and the Past, and from this idea of the three united in one has given us the trinity—Father, Son and Holy Ghost—which was taken from the three-fold deity of the Hindoos, which antedates that of the Jews, who understood the powers of the prism and the breaking of the rays of light into red, yellow and blue, by the means of which they were able to calculate and make astronomical calculations, and with the aid of the triangle, with its three sides in one, they described a part of a circle which represents the infinite and is an important figure in geometry, next in importance to the circle that encloses a globe, which is the most perfect form of all bodies and figures, and represents the whole.

There is no doubt of the great antiquity of the trinity in India, as it is written in books, in a language that has ceased to be spoken for thousands of years, long before the birth of Christ, while in their temples and ruins, in the old cavern of Elephanta, hewn into the solid rock at a time so remote that it is not known in history. Here the traveler beholds with awe and astonishment, in the most conspicuous part of the most ancient and venerable temple of the world, a bust expanding in breadth nearly twenty feet, and no less than eighteen feet in altitude—a bust composed of three heads united to one body, adorned with the oldest symbols of Indian theology, and thus expressly fabricated to indicate the one God in his triune character of the Creator, Preserver and Regenerator of mankind.

The Zoroastrians or sun-worshipers had a trinity in the sun, light, fire, flame, three manifestations of the sun, which gave rise to the all-seeing eye, which is synonymous to that of sun-worship, which Solomon introduced into the order of Freemasonry, which he took from the Egyptians and Assyrians.

The Persian triplicate deity was also composed of three persons—Ormuzd, Mithra and Ahriman.

The Hindoos had three in their trinity, Brahma, Vishnu and Siva, corresponding to power, wisdom and justice, or creator, preserver and destroyer of life, which in their turn answered to spirit, force and matter, and the past, present and future.

The Chinese idol Sampao, consisted of three, equal in all respects.

The ancient Egyptians had their triplet, Emepht, Eicton and Phta; and this triple god, seated on the lotus, one of the images, can now be seen in the St. Petersburg museum.

The Peruvians supposed their god, Tanga-Tanga, to be one in three and three in one.

The ancient Mexicans had also a trinity—Yzona (Father), Bacah (Son) and Echvah (Holy Ghost) and they said they received the doctrine from their ancestors. (See Lord Kingsborough's "Anct. Mex.," page 165.) And these ancient Mexicans or Aztecs had a Christ and a virgin mother; and one of the priests that were with Cortez said that the devil had evidently informed them of these facts, for who else could have given them that information.

All these facts carry us back long anterior to the time mentioned in the old Bible, which was taken by the Egyptians from India, and by the Israelites carried from Egypt to Palestine. Moses and Aaron learned it in the temples from the hierophants or priests, who were learned in all the religious matters, and who guarded their secrets with most sacred vigilance. For centuries the Egyptians were a secluded people like the Chinese, says Herodotus, and the Greeks by stealth drew all their information from them; that the Egyptians were, at an early date, undoubtedly a colony from India, as their religion and civilization bear its ear-marks.

Modern Christanity is nothing but the pure and spiritual doctrines taught by Christ, defiled by paganism and superstition which have been engrafted on it. All the forms and ceremonies that were condemned by Christ had their origin in the old pagan worship of idolatry. The burning of the fire on the altar and the burning of the incense had their origin in the heathen temples thousands of years before the birth of Christ. The nuns of the Roman Catholic church are taken from the vestal virgins, and the monks took the place of the Roman augurs. The forms of churches and cathredals were taken from those of the ancient temples of the heathen gods. These temples were first constructed for tombs, hence the idea is still prevalent of burying the dead in the churchyard or under the church floor or altar.

The *Papal tiara*, which is the crown worn by the Popes of Rome, the so-called successors of St. Peter, is the same as that worn by the gods of ancient Assyria; so also are the tonsure and surplice of the priests copied from the same source, and the tinkling bells were used before the altar of Jupiter Ammon, around the hem of the robe of the high-priest of the Mosaic Jews; and bells were also suspended in the pagodas, and on the sacred table of the Buddhist. The beads and rosaries were used by the Buddhist monks for over five hundred years before the birth of Christ, and the cross was in use for many centuries before it was adopted as a symbol of the Christian church, as a secret sign of recognition among neophytes and adepts of occultism. It is a Kabalistic sign, and represents the oppositions and quaternary equilibrium of the elements. It is also found in the caves and ruins of the prehistoric man of Europe, Asia and America.

The cross, the miter, the dalmatica, the cope which the grand lamas (priests) wear while performing certain ceremonies out of the temple, the service with double choirs, the psalmody, the exorcism, the censer suspended from five chains and which can be opened or closed at pleasure, the benedictions given by the lamas by extending the right hand over the heads of the faithful; the chaplet, ecclesiastical celibacy, religions retirement, the worship of saints, the fasts, the processions, the litanies, the holy water, are all striking analogies that are difficult to explain.

Father Bury, a Portuguese missionary, when he beheld the Chinese bonzes (priests) using rosaries, praying in an unknown tongue and kneeling before images, exclaimed in astonishment, "There is not a piece of dress, not a sacerdotal function, not a ceremony of the courts of Rome which the devil has not copied in this country." (See Kesson, "The Cross and Dragon," also Father Huc's " Recollections of a Journey in Tartary, Thibet and China.")

The question at once rises, which was the original? Did the Christian Catholics copy the Buddhists, or did the Buddhists borrow from them? The rock-cut monasteries and temples in India, the records of China and ,Ceylon, all agree in placing it in favor of the Buddhists, who existed not less than five hundred years before Christ. Says Mr. Hardwicke, " It may have been possible to have two spontaneous growths, but more probable that the one is copied from the other."

The Hindoos had their sacred river in the Ganges, where they bathed and purified themselves; so the Jews had theirs in the river Jordan. The Jews plagiarized their religion from the Hindoos, as the Greeks did from the Egyptians, and the Romans from the Greeks, so that upon a careful scrutiny of all the ancient religions, they bear the ear-marks of one origin in India. And the similiarity of these religions is so great that the modern Hindoos found fault with the British government for allowing a temple of Vishnu to fall to ruins, as they claim that Chrisna and Christ are one and the same person.

Religions, like thoughts, have one common origin in the brain, and in both cases the ideas are more borrowed than original. Symbolism is often used to convey to the untutored mind the idea of some great truth; but frequently the mind cannot yet entirely comprehend it, so that the common mind falls down and worships the image instead of the true being which it is intended to represent. As the mind becomes more enlightened it sees and comprehends these truths and then discards the idols and images and looks up to and feels the great truths in his own mind.

The Madonna is only the reproduction of Isis under a new name, standing on the crescent of the moon, holding her infant Horus in her arms, which represented to the ancient Egyptians that the moon followed the sun, and that Iris, the Earth, with her child Horus, who was the son of Osiris, the sun-god, the ruler of the day, and the son followed the father; that night preceded the day. Juvenal says, "That the painters of Egypt made their living by painting the goddess Isis and her son Horus, and exporting them to Italy, which was a very popular picture at the time of the introduction of Christianity into Rome, and was by the priests substituted for and called the Madonna, the virgin Mary and child." (See "Ten Great Religions," page 254.)

In the explorations of the ancient ruins at Philæ, Upper Egypt, which antedated the birth of Christ, there has been found what was supposed to be the holy family, when in reality it proved to be Osiris, Isis and Horus, instead of being Joseph, Mary and Jesus; and what is still more remarkable, that in the old temples of India they are represented as black, while many of the ancient statues of Buddha are represented with crisp, curly hair, with flat noses and thick lips; nor can it be reasonably doubted that a negro race once held pre-eminence in India. Higgins writes, "There is scarcely an old church in Italy where some remains of the worship of the black virgin and child are not to be met with." This is strong evidence that they were taken either from India or Egypt.

The Holy Communion or Lord's Supper.

The Holy Communion or Lord's Supper had its commencement in the Bacchic mysteries, where a communion cup was handed around after supper, out of which all took a sip of wine. It was called the cup of Agathodæmon. The Orphite rites were similar, where the communion consisted of bread and wine in the worship of nearly every deity of any importance. Epiphanius tells a strange story about a Gnostic sect that celebrated their eucharist, having three vases of the finest and clearest crystal which were filled with white wine, and while the ceremony was going on, in the presence of all, it changed to a blood-red, then a purple, and finally into an azure-blue color. Then the magus handed the vases of wine to a woman of the congregation, asking her to bless it. Then it was poured into a larger vase, and after much prayer and devotion it began to boil and rise in the vase until it ran over.

During the mysteries wine which represented Bacchus was used, he being of Indian origin. Cicero mentioned him as a son of Thyone and Nisus, and consequently Bacchus crowned with ivy or kissos, is Chrisna, one of whose names was Kissen, or Christ. The ancient Greeks and Romans in the mysteries used wine to represent Bacchus and bread for Ceres.

The Deluge.

The ancient Chaldeans and Hindoos had their Adam and Eve, their Noah and the flood, while the Bible would lead us to believe that the Garden of Eden was located on the Euphrates, and that the ark rested on Mount Ararat, while the Hindoo tradition places it on the Himalayas. It cannot be denied that man must have had a beginning, and that there has been a deluge in Central Asia there can be no doubt, the tradition of which can be traced to every country, and which, according to Bunsen, happened about the year 10,000 B. C., and had nought to do with the mythical Noah or Nuah. A partial cataclysm occurs at the close of every geological "age" of the world, which does not destroy it, but only changes its general appearance. While some portions are submerged, others are elevated. And the fossils found lead us to believe that new races of men, new animals and a new flora evolve from the dissolution of the preceding ones.

The Hindoo tradition says that Vaivasvata, who in the Bible becomes Noah, was saved by a little fish, which turned out to be an avater of Vishnu. The fish warns that just man that the globe is about to be submerged, that all the inhabitants must perish, and orders him to construct a vessel in which he shall embark with all his family. When the ship is finished he goes on board with his entire family, taking with him the seeds of all plants and a pair of every kind of animal; then the heavens open and the rains fall and the entire surface of the earth is covered with water A gigantic fish, armed with a horn, places itself at the head of the ark, and the holy man, following its orders, attaches a cable to its horn, and the fish guides the ship for forty days and nights through the raging elements, and finally landed the ark on the summit of the Himalayas; yet among all the ancient Egyptian writings there is no mention of a deluge, therefore it is evident that it was confined to Central Asia, if it ever occurred at all, and as the writings of the ancient Hindoos are much older than those o' the Bible, it most probably was taken from the Hindoo by the Chaldeans, and from them by the Jews. But it is, in all probability, an allegory representing the incarnation of the spirit in the flesh

Noah is the Chaldean for Nuah, who is the king of the humid principle, the spirit moving or floating on the waters in his ark, the latter being the emblem of the argha or moon, the feminine principle. Noah is the "spirit" falling into matter, so we find him as soon as he descended to the earth, planting a vineyard, drinking wine and getting drunk on it, i e , the pure spirit becoming intoxicated as soon as it is finally imprisoned in matter

The dagon or fish-man, found engraven in stone and metal of the ancients, had its origin in the idea that man sprang from fish. The Japanese have a singular idol formed out of the body and tail of a fish, fastened upon the head and shoulders of a monkey, which gave rise to the idea of mermaids "The Hindoo god, Vishnu, assumed the form of a fish with a human head, in order to reclaim the Vedas, lost during the deluge. Having enabled Visvamitra to escape with all his tribe in the ark, but, pitying weak and erring humanity, he remained with them for some time, taught them how to build houses and cultivate the land He remained on land in the day-time and went to the ocean to pass his nights. "One day he plunged into the water and returned no more, for the earth had covered itself with vegetation, fruit and cattle."

This fable of Vishnu disguised as a fish gives weight to the sacred books of the Hindoos, especially in view of the fact that the Vedas and Manu reckon more than twenty-five thousand years of existence, as proved by the most serious as well as the most authentic documents Few people, says the learned Halhed, have their annals more authentic or more serious than the Hindoos.

The big story of Jonah and the whale had its origin in the same idea, that man sprang from out of the fish. Vishnu is evidently the Adam Kadmon of the Kabalists, for Adam is the Logos, or the first anointed, as Adam second is the King Messiah; Adam Kadmon was an emanation of Jehovah, and Adam the first man was the first materialized spirit of man clothed in flesh; having lost the power to dematerialize was forced to live in the flesh on the earth. Being androgynous, as all angels are, and falling into deep sleep or trance, the female principle was separated by drawing her life principle out of his side and materialized in the maternal form of a woman, called Eve in the Bible

Lakmy, or Lakshmi, the passive or female counterpart of Vishnu, the creator and preserver, is also called Ada Maya. She is the "mother of the world," Damatri, the Venus aphrodite of the Greeks; she is also called Isis and Eve. While Venus was born from the sea-foam, Lakmy springs out from the water at the churning of the sea When born she is so beautiful that all the gods fall in love with her. The Jews, borrowing their types wherever they could get them, made their first woman after the pattern of Lakmy It is a curious coincidence that Viracocha, the Supreme Being of ancient Peru, means, when literally translated, "foam of the sea "

In the oldest Hindoo book, Manu, there is a passage that says, "That this world issued out of darkness, the subtle elementary principles produced the vegetable seed, which animated first the plants From plants, life passed into fantastical bodies, which were born in the waters; then, through a series of forms of plants, worms, insects, fish, serpents, tortoises, cattle and wild animals, until finally man was evolved. This is in accordauce with the laws of evolution, as laid down by Darwin and Huxley.

"The object of all religions," says the Persian Hafiz, "is alike." All men seek their beloved, and is not all the world love's dwelling? Why talk of a mosque or a church?

Hindoo teachers say, "The creed of the lover differs from other creeds God is the creed of those who love Him, and to do good is best with the followers of every faith." He alone is a true Hindoo whose heart is just, and he only is a good Mussulman whose life is pure. "Remember Him who has seen numberless Mahomets, Vishnus, Vivas, come and go, and who is not found by one who forgets or turns from the poor." "The common standpoint of the three religions," says the Chinese, "is that they insist on the banishment of evil desire and do good."

So we see in all religious beliefs a commingling of their forms and ceremonies, which goes far to establish the fact that all religions must have had their origin from a belief in a state of future existence.

CHAPTER XI

COMPARATIVE THEOLOGY, like comparative anatomy, comparative geography, and comparative philology, is yet in its infancy It is a science which consists in the study of the facts of human history and their relation to each other. It does not dogmatize; it observes, and it deals only with phenomena and facts that relate to the spiritual nature in man

By comparing the various religions of mankind we see wherein they differ, wherein they agree, and what appears true and what false It shows both sides of religion and that as it has advanced with civilization, it has lost much of its severity, and that a higher religion and better morals must find root in the decaying soils of past religious beliefs and traditions of God, duty and immortality of the soul

The duty of comparative theology is to do justice to all the religions of mankind, to strike out all debasing superstitions and arrive at the truth. All religions teach the immortality of the soul, future rewards and punishments, a hell and a heaven The basis of all religions is spiritism; that the spirit of the departed lives and has its existence in the atmosphere surrounding us

The ablest writers on comparative theology are Max Muller, Bunsen, Burnouf, Dollinger, Hardwicke, St. Hilaire, Duncker, Baur, Renan, Cox, and J F. Clarke, author of the "Ten Great Religions" These writers show great learning and have stripped mythology and theology of its outward forms and sacred robes, showing, beyond a doubt, that religions, like civilizations, are the outgrowth of older religions and civilizations, that it comes from within; that it is a part of man's nature to be religious, so that he has often been called a religious animal, as no other animal offers up prayers or supplications to the Great Spirit of the unseen universe

All the principal religions, like the human race, appear to have had their origin in Asia, and have spread thence over the whole civilized world Each race has adopted a certain religion that has had much to do in shaping its civilization Research has shown that India is the mother of civilization and religion; that, far back in the night of time, the songs of the Reg-Veda were written in Sanscrit It is the oldest written language, and is the mother of the Greek language, which, from its perfection, was claimed by the Greeks as the language of the gods—while the modern Christians, adhering to the idea of Moses and creation, make the Hebrew the language of God as given to Adam and Eve in the Garden of Eden

There appears to be a material connection between language and religion. As language is the medium through which the soul communicates its thoughts and feelings to its fellow-man, so, in the growth and development of language, we are enabled to trace the early ideas and views of primitive man far back in the past, long before there was ever a written language, for words were used long before they were reduced to writing, so that the philologist is enabled to trace back the Aryan religion to a period long before it separated into different races So that by the use of words, generic in their nature, that are to be found in common use, by different races speaking different languages—the same or similar words are used to express the same thing or ideas—it is evident that far back in the past these different races spoke a common language; and when the generic words relate to God or religion, then it is evidence that their religion was about the same. So in this way the human family has been traced back to the different origins and centers from which it diverged. Each of these diverging races carries with them these generic words, with their meaning about the same, though they may and often do change the nomenclature of these generic words, as the dialects and provincialisms tend to give the phonetic sounds to them.

"It," says Max Muller, "we would learn to be charitable in the interpretation of the language of other religions, we shall more easily learn to be charitable in the interpretation of our own language. We shall no longer try to force a literal interpretation on words and sentences in our sacred books, which, if interpreted literally, must lose their original purport and their spiritual truth." If we can make allowance for mouth and lips and breath, we can surely make the same allowance for words and their utterance, for all languages have their dialects. There is a high and there is a low dialect; there is a broad and there is a narrow dialect; there are dialects for men and for women and for children; for clergy and for laity; for the noisy streets and for the still and quiet life of the closets of students; and as the child advances to manhood it has to learn its language and its religion.

The religion of the nursery, with baby talk, ghost and witch stories, implants a superstitious religion which requires a severe mental struggle to outgrow, and some are so effeminate that they never are able to throw it off. Therefore the mass of mankind speak the language of their fathers and adopt their ideas of politics and business, and cling to the religion of their mother; therefore the masses move slowly in politics and still slower in religion. The early expressions of religion were no doubt frequently childish and mythical, which has tended to confuse the scholar in arriving at what was the real religious sentiment. It is impossible to express abstract ideas except by metaphor, and it is not too much to say that the whole dictionary of ancient religion is made up of metaphors, and consequently there is a constant struggle in the mind to free the material from the spiritual.

By the aid of comparative philology man has been enabled to trace the leading races and religions back to three centers in Asia—the Aryan, the Semitic and the Turanic. The Aryan includes the Hindoo and the European races, for that reason they are called Indo-European, and some call them the Indo-Germanic. I am inclined to believe Indo-European is, perhaps, the best term, as it leads to less confusion. This race at a very early date broke up into four parts. The Indians or Hindoos went southeast into India by the way of the Punjaub, while the Iranians settled in Persia, and reach through Hindoo Koos mountains east to the country now known as Afghanistan, and to the Himalaya mountains, and west into the Caucasus mountains, which was at one time supposed to be the home of the white race, who are often called the Caucausian race. The Greeks and Romans entered Europe by crossing the Hellespont. Æneas fled from Troy and settled in Italy. The Celts, Teutons and Sclavs entered Europe from the north side of the Black Sea.

The Hindoo branch of the Aryan family still adheres to its old religion, and in the belief of spirits and of the spirituality of God in the shape of a Divine mind or Sensorium, from whence all divine intelligence is drawn. And their religion is that of Brahminism and Buddhism. Their sacred books or bible is the Vedas, written in the Sanscrit, and from this language the philologist is enabled to trace the origin of the Greek, Latin, and the German and Anglo-Saxon and English languages.

It is evident that the Semitic religion of Abraham dates far back into the past, long, before the flood, which was the submerging of some portion of the Eastern hemisphere, perhaps a submerged continent which is now called Lemuria. It lies to the south of India, and is where some writers locate the origin of man on earth.

The Bible says, "And Joshua said unto all the people; thus saith the Lord God of Israel: your fathers dwelt on the other side of the flood in old times, even Terah, the father of Abraham and the father of Nachor, and they served other gods. * * * Now, therefore, fear the Lord and serve Him in sincerity and truth; and put away the gods which your fathers served on the other side of the flood and in Egypt and serve ye the Lord."

And it is evident from this declaration of Joshua that before the flood they had other gods, and it might have been that they belonged to the same stock or root as the Aryan races, who had many gods. The Brahmins claim that they got their knowledge of God from the Pitri, who lived before the flood. They were spirits who returned to earth to teach man after the flood. Here we get a glimpse of the remoteness of man and his religion, and here was the beginning of the Hebrew race and religion; the idea of a Jehovah and a jealous, revengeful God, a monotheisthic God without wife or children, to whom Christianity has given a son equal to the father, and Mohammedanism has given Him a prophet who has charge of His earthly affairs and of the admission into Paradise.

The Semitic nations have, on the contrary, a different word for their deity, *El*, which means strong, and throughout all the Semitic races it is a term applied to their deity. In the Hebrew we have the word *Beth-El*, the house of God; *ha-El*, the strong one.

"El was the name for God in Babylon, and was worshiped at Byblis by the Phœnicians, and he was called the sun of heaven and earth. His father was the son of *Elium*, the most high God, who had been killed by wild animals. The son of Elium, who succeeded him, was dethroned and at last slain by his own son El, whom Philo identified with the Greek Kronos, and is represented as the presiding deity of the planet Saturn, with the name of El. Philo connected the name with Elohim, the plural of *Eloah*. In the battle between El and his father, the aliens of El, he says, 'were called Elohim, as those who were with Kronos were called Kronivi.'"

Eloah is used in the Bible synonymous with El. It means gods in general or false gods, while in Arabic *ilah* without the article means a god in general, with the article Al-ilah or Allah becomes the name of the God of Mohammed. Hence we find through all the Semitic races different terms for God, which have been changed but little from El, the Babylonian name for God.

The majority of the writers of philology claim that the Semitic language had its origin in a different root. That it sprang from some wild, ape-like man family or group, far different from that of the Aryan.

Elyon, which in Greek means the highest, is used in the old Testament as a predicate of God. It occurs also by itself as a name of Jehovah. Melchizedek is called emphatically the priest of El-Elyon—the priest of the Most High God. It is evidently derived from a Phœnician word, Elium, the High God, the Father of Heaven, who was the father of El. The word Jehovah or Jahveh is supposed to be derived from a Chaldean word, Ido, God. It is claimed by Sir Henry Rawlinson to be found on inscriptions in the ruins of Babylon. Yet it may be of Hebrew origin—after their separation from the main branch of the Semitic race—and, therefore was a local word, which the Jews used in the sense of the one true God. Abraham worshiped God as Jehovah, and philologists differ as to whether it is of Hebrew origin.

The Semitic nations, Assyrians, Babylonians, Phœnicians, Carthagenians, the Moabites, Philistians, and, sometimes, the Jews, called their great or supreme God, Bel, or Baal. Before the flood, he was called Bel. Though originally *one* Baal, he became divided into many divine personalities through the influence of local worship. So we hear of a Baal-tsur, Baal-tsidon, Baal-tare, originally the Baal of Tyre, of Sidon, and of Tarsus. At Shechem, Baal was worshiped as Baal-barith, supposed to mean the God of treaties. At Ekron, the Philistians worshiped him as Baal-zebub, the lord of flies (hence comes our Beelzebub); while the Moabites, and the Jews, too, knew him also by the name of Baal-peor. On the Phœnician coins, Baal is called Baal-shamayim, the Baal of heaven, which is the Beelsamen of Philo, identified by him with the sun, and makes him a *sun-god*.

When the ancient Babylonians spoke of Belus, the Supreme God, cutting off his own head, that the blood flowing from it might be mixed with the dust out of which men were formed, sounds horrible and absurd; but, by this myth, they only convey the idea that there is in man an element of divine life—that we are also his offspring. The ancient Egyptians convey about the same idea in the seventeenth chapter of thier "ritual," that the sun mutilated himself, and that from the stream of his blood he created beings. And Moses conveys the same idea in Genesis when he says that, "God formed man from the dust of the ground, and breathed into his nostrils the breath of life"

The Assyrians, Babylonians, Phœnicians, Hebrews, Syrian tribes, Arabs and Carthagenians all belonged to the Semitic race. It is the only race that was ever a rival of the Aryan race. The Semitic race has been great on land and sea From the valley of the Euphrates and that of the Tigris, its sons carried their peculiar civilization west to the Mediterranean sea, whose commerce at one time was under the control of the Phœnicians, whose ships explored the coast and made settlements at Carthage and Cadiz, and sailed as far north as Great Britain, and circumnavigated Africa two thousand years before Vasco de Gama

The languages of the Semitic nations is very closely related, being almost the dialects of a single tongue, the difference between them being hardly greater than between the different dialects of the German race

The Phœnician language is almost identical with that of the Hebrew, and the Phœnicians had the Jewish love of commerce, trade, and making money. By some historians they have been called the ancient Jews of the Mediterranean This race has given to man the alphabet, the Bible, the Koran, commerce, and the greatest military genius of the past, Hannibal.

The peculiarities of these races have been in the structure of their language and the forms of their religion, which consisted mainly of monotheism—a belief in the existence of one personal God only—while the belief of the Aryan races was that of polytheism—a belief in the plurality of the gods or invisible beings superior to man, and having an agency in the government of the world, and who could assist mortals, a kind of ancestral worship of the spirits of ancestors, friends, heroes and statesmen, who became gods

"The highest God [of the Aryans] received the same name in the ancient mythology of India, Greece, Italy and Germany, and they retained that name, whether worshiped on the Himalayan mountains (Olympus) or among the oaks of Dodona, on the Capitol, or in the forest of Germany * * * We have in the Vedas the invocation *Dyans-pitar*, the Greek, *Ya-he created*, the Latin *Jupiter*, which means in all three languages what it meant before these languages were torn asunder—it means HEAVENLY FATHER. It did not mean idolatry, or nature-worship, but the Great Spirit that dwelt in the sky, the source of all life and light, from which all intelligence and good has emanated" (See Max Muller's "Science of Religion")

The ancient Greek and Roman religion is evidently of Aryan origin, as it is illustrated in Homer, Hesiod and Virgil They believed in tutelary and ancestral spirits, though their religion had become much mixed with that of Egypt and with the Semitic religion, which they introduced into their mythology.

There have been two streams of religion flowing through two channels, one the Aryan and the other the Semitic; one from the plains of the Euphrates to the Jordan and to the Mediterranean, while the other has flown from the Indus to the Thames, through the middle of Europe, among the blonde race, while the former has been engrafted in the dark races in the south of Europe, in a modified form of the monotheistic Semitic religion — the Roman Catholic religion

While, in a still more modified form, it has spread over the whole of middle and northern Europe, where it is known as Protestantism, which is more liberal in its views and loses much of its monotheistic nature and becomes more spiritual. The anthropomorphic idea of an individual God meets with but little favor from the Indo-Germanic races, who are fast falling into the spiritual belief, which was the original religion of the Aryan race, before it became engrafted on Christianity, which was a departure from the monotheistic belief of the Semitic races As the Christian religion is more Brahminical than Mosaical, it is a reincarnation of Chrisna or Buddha, and it is more humane and not tyrannical, like that of the Mosaic.

The Hindoo branch of the Aryan family, like the Hebrew branch of the Semitic family, has produced two religious books, or two religions, one being the outgrowth of the other. The Hindoos have given rise to Brahminism, and Buddhism is its outgrowth. The Hebrew religion had its origin in Mosaicism, and its outgrowth is Christianity. The Irænians—the ancient Persians—a branch of the Aryan race, had another religion known as Zoroasterism, which is found in the Zend-Avesta, and draws much from the old Vedas, the sacred books of the Brahmins. There is still another branch of the Semitic race, the Arabs, which has given to the world another religion known as Mohammedanism, the outgrowth of the old Bible, or rather the old Testament, which has respect for Christ as a prophet, but differs with Christianity as to his divine origin

The old monotheisthic doctrine of Moses, taught in the old Testament, that there is but one God and Moses is his prophet, is now embraced by the entire Semitic race, so that practically this race has again returned to its original belief in one God—a man-like God, as Moses says, "God created man in his own image," and it can therefore be claimed that he is in the shape and form of a *man*, and this man-like God punishes as well as offers rewards and grants forgiveness of sin through the influence of the Prophet So thousands flock to Mecca, as Christians do to Jerusalem, to do homage to these sacred places.

Christianity was an improvement on Mosaicism; so was Buddhism an improvement on Brahminism; and both tended to purify and better the condition of the religious sentiment of the people. Christ, though a Jew, was rejected by the Jews, but his religious sentiment found lodgment among the gentiles—the Indo-European races—but never was very palatable to the Semitic races, which clung to the monotheistic idea of a man-like God The doctrine of the trinity was something they could never comprehend, and so they readily fell into the Mohammedan religion, as enunciated by its great prophet, who said, "There is but one God and Mohammed is his prophet," while the Jews claim there is but one God and Moses is his prophet.

The Assyrians, Babylonians, Phœnicians and Carthagenians had a similar religion. They believed in a Supreme God, called by different names—Ira, Bel, Set, Hadad, Moloch, Chemosh, Jaoh El, Adon and Asshur. All believed in subordinate and secondary beings emanating from this Supreme Being, who were his manifestations to the world, and who were the rulers of the planets. Like other pantheistic religions, the custom prevailed among the Semitic nations of promoting first one and then the other deity to be the supreme object of worship. Among the Assyrians, as among the Egyptians, the gods were often arranged in triads, as that of Anu, Bel and Ao Anu or Aannes wore the head of a fish, Bel wore the horns of a bull, and Ao was represented by a serpent Moses is frequently represented as having a ram's horn on the side of his head.

Brahminism, like the Church of Rome, es. tablished a system of sacramental salvation in the hands of a sacred order. Buddhism, like Protestantism, revolted and established a doctrine of individual salvation, based on personal character. Brahminism, like the Church of Rome, teaches an exclusive Spiritualism, glorifying penances and martyrdom, and considers the body the enemy of the soul But Buddhism and Protestantism accept nature and its laws, and make it a religion of humanity as well as of devotion. There may be some exceptions, but the rule generally applies

The Roman Catholic Church and Brahminism place the essence of religion in sacrifices. The daily sacrifice of mass is the central feature of the former, while Protestantism and Buddhism save the soul by teaching. In the Roman Church the sermon is subordinate to mass, while in Protestantism and Buddhism sermons are the main instruments by which souls are saved

Brahminism is a system of inflexible castes; the priestly order is made distinct and supreme. So in Romanism the priesthood alone constitute the church, while in Buddhism and Protestantism the laity regain their rights. Buddhism in Asia, like Protestantism in Europe and America, is a revolt of nature against spirit, of humanity against caste, of individual freedom against the despotism of an order, of salvation by faith against salvation by sacrament.

While Buddhism is often called the Protestantism of the East, it has many of the forms and ceremonies of Romanism. The chanting of prayers, counting of beads, burning of incense and candles before the image of the virgin Mary, called the queen of heaven, having an infant in her arms and holding a cross. While Buddhism makes God or the good and heaven to be equivalent to nothing or repose, it intensifies and exaggerates evil. Though heaven is a blank, hell is a very solid reality. It is present and future too; everything in the thousand hells of Buddhism is painted as vividly as in the hell of Dantes. God has disappeared from the universe and in his place is only the inexorable law, which grinds on forever. It punishes and rewards, but has no love in it. It is only dead, cold, hard, cruel, unrelenting law. Yet Buddhists are not atheists any more than a child who has never heard of God. A child cannot be either deist or atheist, because it has no theology.

The platonic philosophy was able to grasp and hold the idea of God and man, the infinite and finite, the eternal and the temporal. Christianity recognizes God as the infinite and eternal, but recognizes also the world of time and space as real. Man exists as well as God; we love God, we must love man too. Brahminism loves God, but not man; it has piety, but no humanity. Buddhism loves man, but not God; it has humanity, no piety; if it has piety it is by a beautiful want of logic, its heart being wiser than its head.

Christianity takes all the good there is in the Buddhist doctrine and gives man a live God, a soul, a heaven, and a hereafter. Buddhism makes man struggle up to God, while Christianity makes God come down to man, and unites all in one vast brotherhood.

For further information I refer you to the "Esoteric Buddhism," by Sinnett:

"The one universal spirit comprehending eternal matter, motion, space and duration, evolves the boundless cosmos, comprising countless solar systems, each consisting of seven planetary chains of seven planets each.

"Evolution takes a like course through each planetary chain, the members of which are intimately bound together by subtile currents and forces. The passage of individual spiritual entities round this chain constitutes the evolution of man, which is still in progress. There are seven kingdoms of nature. Of the three lowest Western science knows nothing. The mineral, vegetable, animal and man complete the list, the latter including beings of higher

organization than we are yet familiar with. The wave of existence makes seven rounds through the planetary chain, each sphere being fitted for a different phase of progress, regarding both animate and inanimate nature. Darwin's 'Missing Link' is picked up here. Man, whose destiny is the principal object of inquiry, on each round develops in each sphere seven great root races, each producing seven sub-races, again divided into seven branches, and it is well enough to know that we are of the fourth round, fifth race and seventh sub-race; or, in other words, just beyond the middle point of our cyclic career. Considering that the individual nomad makes its progress by successive incarnations of not less than two to each branch race, and that the evolution of our present root-race began about one million years ago, the magnitude and duration of the scheme begins to dawn upon the mind, and on learning that beyond the seven rounds of each planetary chain lies the solar, and beyond that universal cycle, imagination retires baffled from the attempt to realize the plan.

"Seven distinct principles enter into the constitution of man; the body, vitality, the astral body, the animal soul, the human soul, the spiritual soul, and spirit. The first needs no explanation. The second is matter in its aspect as force. Though immaterial, its affinity for gross matter prevents its separation from it except by instant translation to some other particle or mass. We get the idea in the modern theory of the 'Persistence of Force.' The astral body is the eternal duplicate of the physical body—its original design. It guides vitality in its work on the physical particles, and causes it to build up the shape which these assume. Query: Has this any bearing on that stumbling block of modern biology, the subsequent determination of apparently identical embryos? These three lower principles are of the earth earthy, perishable in their nature as a single entity, and done with by man at his death. The animal soul is the first of the principles which attaches to man's higher nature. It is the seat of the desires and the vehicle of will, influencing, and influenced by the fifth principle, the human soul. This is the seat of reason and memory, and in the majority of mankind is not yet fully developed.

It follows as a matter of course that the sixth principle, the spiritual soul, is yet in embyro. Yet the sixth and also the seventh principle, or pure spirit, inheres in man's nature, and the human soul is capable of assimilating them in its progress to perfection. This seven-fold nature of man is the key to his destiny. At death the three lower principles are finally abandoned by that which is really man himself, the Ego, and the remaining principles escape to Devachan, the world of spirits. A contest ensues, the fourth principle drawing the fifth earthward, while the sixth and seventh attract it upward. The lower instincts, impulses and recollections of the fifth adhere to the fourth, while its most elevated and spiritual portions cling to the sixth and seventh. Devachan is a *state*, not a locality, in which the soul experiences a subjective existence. The karma of physical existence, that is, the affinities for good and evil, generated by man during objective life, determine the duration and character of the subjective life. Like earthly existence it has its season of infancy, prime and exhaustion, passing through oblivion, not into death, but birth, reincarnation and the resumption of action which begets a new karma, to be worked out in another term of devachan. So the process goes on from race to race, from sphere to sphere, from round to round, until perfected humanity attains its destiny in the repose of Nirvana; not the Nirvana of popular misconception—annihilation—but the sublime state of conscious rest in Omniscience. 'The dewdrop slips into the shining sea.'

"Fantastic and absurd as much of this 'Theory of Nature' may appear, it cannot fail in some respects to arouse earnest attention. Is it nothing that ancient religion and modern science clasp hands across the interval of thirty centuries?

"The most prominent and yet unsettled theories of modern thought, the nebular hypothesis, evolution, the descent of man, dubious problems in biology, ethnology and kindred sciences are incorporated with and made a part of an ancient religo-philosophic system, and besides the grand sweep of these Oriental generalizations, the speculations of modern science seems timid, tentative and feeble.

"Is it possible that our Western civilization does not embrace all that is known of nature and man? That along other lines of inquiry, and following methods strange and unsatisfactory to us, other men have through centuries pushed their investigations and stored up the results in the archives of secret associations; and that now, when modern thought, released from mediæval fetters, is preparing the way for the recognition of truths in nature, hitherto unknown or denounced, these stores are to be opened to our view to prove the coherence of all truth?"

The religions of Persia, Egypt, Greece and Rome have come to an end, having shared the fate of their civilization, and while Brahma, Buddha, India and Islam have been arrested, Christianity has taken a milder form, and a new religion called modern Spiritualism has sprung up, which in the last quarter of a century has spread over the whole civilized world, making inroads upon all other religions. It now numbers not less than twenty-five millions, of the most intelligent advanced thinkers of the age, while the Christian religions vary from one hundred and twenty to one hundred and seventy millions, the Buddhist from two hundred and twenty-two to three hundred and twenty millions, the Mohammedans from one hundred and ten to one hundred and sixty millions, the Brahmins from one hundred and eleven to one hundred and thirty millions, the Jews from four to six millions. That of the Chinese religions we have no figures to go by.

M. Hubner gives the following religious statistics, comprising the leading religions of the world:

CHRISTIANS, 400,000,000.

Roman Catholics	200,000,000
Protestants	110,000,000
Greeks	80,000,000
Various other sects	10,000,000

NON-CHRISTIANS, 992,500,000.

Buddhists	500,000,000
Brahmins	150,000,000
Mohammedans	80,000,000
Israelites	6,500,000
Unknown different religions	240,000,000
Unknown religions	16,000,000
Total	1,392,500,000

It is generally conceded that the teachings of Confucius, which are rather a philosophy than a religion, are among the oldest we have record of, while that of Lao-tse and Tao-ism, its contemporary, was founded on that of spiritism. Herodotus, who traveled in Egypt 450 B. C., gives us an account of the monuments in that country, in which were found China ware, with Chinese mottos, which Rosellini believes to have been imported from China by kings contemporary with or before the time of Moses. There have been similar vases found in the ruins of Troy, that go to prove that China was a highly civilized nation long before the siege of Troy, and if Chinese history is to be relied on, it will take us back into the gray mist of the past some twenty-five thousand years, and it is now generally admitted that Confucius lived at least five hundred and fifty hears before the Christian era.

Chronologists differ as to which is the oldest civilization, Egypt or India. The Greeks and Romans trace back to Egypt, and for a long period of time it was thought that Egypt was the cradle of civilization. But learned philologists and ethnologists contend that India is the oldest in the arts and has the oldest religions. Others again claim that they are different and, perhaps, spontaneous developments. Plato gives us an intimation that the Egyptians had knowledge of the submerged continent of Atlantis. And from the similarity of the temples and pyramids in Central America it might have been possible, at a very remote period, that these countries had intercourse with each other.

Every religion has been an outgrowth of preceding religious faiths. Back of all religions and civilizations there is an older religion and civilization. Palestine had been colonized by Arab tribes from Idumea and Phœnicia long before it was invaded by the children of Israel under the leadership of Joshua and Moses. Eventually they became more or less consolidated as the kingdoms of Samaria and Judea. Their fables, legends, traditions and family religions were more or less amalgamated and nationalized under the name of Judea.

"The greater part of the gods of all nations were ancient heroes, famous for their achievements and their worthy deeds, and were such as kings, generals and founders of cities. To these some added the splendid and useful objects in the natural world, as the sun, moon and stars, and some were not ashamed to pay divine honors to mountains, rivers, trees, etc. The worship of these deities consisted in ceremonies, sacrifices and prayers. The ceremonies were for the most part absurd and ridiculous, and thoroughly debasing, obscene and cruel. The prayers were truly insipid and void of piety, both in form and matter. The priests who presided over this worship basely abused their authority to impose on the people. The whole pagan system had not the least efficacy to produce and cherish virtuous emotions in the soul, because the gods and goddesses were patterns of vice, and the priests bad men, and the doctrines false." (See Mosheim's "Church History.")

The narrow creeds excluding God, the Father, from any communication with the great majority of human beings, is revolting to common sense and humanity. Selecting a few of his chosen children to be saved and leaving the rest to perish in their ignorance, is an extremely selfish view of an intelligent God. He caused some to be born in India, some in China, and others in Europe, Africa, America, and in the far-distant islands of the sea; they are all His children and they are all as dear to him as are the Jews. He speaks to each of them through the same channel, whether he be a Brahmin, Buddhist, Chinese, Mohammedan, Christian, pagan or heathen; "In Him we live and move and have our being." He is above all, and through all, and in all.

"Abraham," says Max Muller, "was the first we have any record of who could raise his soul to the contemplation of a Perfect Being above all, and the source of all. With passionate love he adored this Most High God, maker of heaven and earth." The mind of Abraham rose to a clear conception of the unity of God as excluding all other divine beings; yet if we will examine the expressions of this great Arab chief, as described in the book of Genesis, we can see at once that he was a great medium and a theosophist, who held converse with the spirits, the same as our modern mediums. When they told him to sacrifice his son Isaac he was ready to do it under the firm belief that it was the voice of God, when he heard another voice that told him not to kill Isaac, that there was a ram tangled in the vines near by. This was a clear case of clair-audience.

Mr. Renan says the Indo-European race, distracted by the variety of the universe, never by itself arrived at monotheism. The Semitic race, on the other hand, guided by its firm and sure sight, instantly unmasked divinity, and without reflection or reasoning attained the purest form of religion that humanity has ever known. The Hebrews, like the Assyrians and Babylonians, were divided between monothe-ism and sabacism or star-worship. The Se-mitic, like the Aryan races, had a confused idea of one Supreme God behind all the sec-ondary deities.

Pure monotheism appears to be a direct reve-lation to Moses; and even in Jehovah we are led to believe that Moses gave him more of the attributes of a big Moses or man than that of an All Wise and Supreme God.

Christianity, as soon as it became the reli-gion of a no-Semitic race, lost much of its mo-notheism and tended to pantheism. They added to God "all above," and the God "with all," the God "in us all." The new Testament is full of this kind of pantheism, God in man as well as God with man. Jesus made the step forward from God with man to God in man; "I am in them, thou in me." The doctrine of the Holy Spirit is this idea of God, who is not only will and power, not only wisdom and law, but love of God, who desires communion and intercourse with his children, and who, therefore, comes and dwells with them. Mohammed teaches a God above us; Moses teaches a God above us and yet with us; Jesus teaches God above us, God with us and God in us.

Christianity teaches of a Supreme Being who is a pure *spirit*. It is a more spiritual religion than Brahminism, for the latter has passed on into polytheism and idolatry. Christianity is more flexible and is more capable of becoming able to supply the religious wants of all races of men, therefore it is fitted to become the universal religion of man, it being a composite made up of all the previous religions; and con-sequently it is an improvement on all the other religions.

Jesus Christ was a man born a seer, a pro-phet and endowed with remarkable mediumis-tic gifts, which were improved by development by the assistance of the spirits. He was mis-understood by his immediate followers, and was imputed to be something superior to man, and his deeds were exaggerated by their unrea-soning credulity. Elevated above the multi-tude by his superior spirituality, he was quali-fied to be a teacher of the sublime inspirations which flowed into his receptive mind from wise and pure spirits, who made him their mouth-piece to the masses. Pure and spiritual in his life, he was prepared for rapid progress as a spirit; and now, with other ancient prophets and exalted men, he holds a place among celes-tial spirits, having experienced his second spir-itual birth and become a dweller in the third sphere.

Peter, in Acts ii: 22, says: "I see in Jesus of Nazareth a *man* approved of by God among you by miracles, wonders and signs that God did in him." "I and my father are one;" one in purpose, one in spirit. He worshiped in spirit, and he never lost sight of the spiritual world. God did not speak to him from with-out. He feels that God is in him. He needed no sound of thunder, like Moses; no revealing tempest, like Job; no familiar oracle, like the Grecian sage; but he consciously lived in and with the Father in the spiritual, as he was *en rapport* with the Divine mind, which permeated all the whole universe. If man would live as Christ directed, and in harmony with natural laws, he could converse with angels (spirits) as they did in the days of Abraham, Christ and the apostles.